PERSONALLY SPEAKING

PERSONALLY SPEAKING

SELECTIONS FROM THE WRITINGS OF

DR. RALPH C. SMEDLEY

FOUNDER OF TOASTMASTERS INTERNATIONAL, INC.

IN MEMORIAM

1878-1965

Published by TOASTMASTERS INTERNATIONAL, Santa Ana, California

PERSONALLY
SPEAKING

Selections and commentary:
Dr. Seth A. Fessenden
Chairman, Dept. of Speech
California State
University-Fullerton

Editor: Maurice Forley
Executive Director
Toastmasters International

Foreword

When Dr. Ralph C. Smedley launched the first Toastmasters Club back in 1924, did he envision the tremendous growth the movement would take worldwide? Over thirty years later, Dr. Smedley did recognize that, as communication crucially affected "almost every phase of life," the Toastmasters "process had values far beyond the mere training" of people to "face audiences and speak their ideas."

Today, with as many as 130,000 members in 6000 clubs throughout more than 50 countries, the organization that sprang from Dr. Smedley's ideas and ideals flourishes.

What were those fertile ideas and ideals? Dr. Smedley promoted the principles of learning by doing and improving through practice and evaluation. He taught that participants "be encouraged to develop and use their own initiative and originality for their own improvement."

Dr. Smedley drew inspiration from the belief that communication is a gift "to be used by all for the good of all." He sought to apply this gift to the "building of a better society made up of individuals who must act in groups."

Above all, Dr. Smedley stressed the importance of personal relationships to the health of the Toastmasters program. Without personal relationships, he said, "we might easily become just another high-grade correspondence school."

Dr. Smedley also emphasized the power of simplicity. This brings us back to our original question about the scope of his founding of Toastmasters. According to Dr. Smedley, he did not envision the tremendous growth into such an eminent organization. His motivation was simply to "meet a local need," the "very evident need for practical help in the art of communication."

It is with the same spirit of meeting needs in a practical, personal way that we offer you, the reader, these gleanings from Dr. Smedley's teachings.

The words preserved in this collection are Dr. Smedley's own. The Toastmasters he originally addressed were an all-male group. Therefore, Dr. Smedley used the generic term "man" and the masculine third person pronoun exclusively.

Today, Toastmasters welcomes women into its clubs as well as men. Our reproduction of Dr. Smedley's authentic words in no way compromises our current policy of open membership. We hope that all readers, male and female, benefit from Dr. Smedley's teachings as intended, as directed to them personally.

Let Dr. Smedley introduce himself to you through the grace and sincerity of his words. These words remain as luminous witness to the warmth and insight of the man.

We in Toastmasters treasure them as a rich inheritance, and invite you to be enriched by them, too.

The Ralph C. Smedley Memorial Fund

Keep The Legacy Alive

"Education is our business. It has been so from the beginning." This is how Dr. Smedley explained his vision for Toastmasters International. To help advance its founder's commitment to education, the organization has established the Ralph C. Smedley Memorial Fund.

The Smedley Fund is an opportunity to contribute to the creation and promotion of learning materials in the field of communication and leadership. It provides financial support to researchers and consultants actively engaged in developing new means and methods of education.

To find out how you can participate in the Smedley Fund program, contact Toastmasters International World Headquarters: 2200 North Grand Avenue, P.O. Box 10400, Santa Ana, California 92711 U.S.A. (714) 542-6793.

The deepest joy of belonging
comes as one learns to cooperate,
contribute, and help...

Dr. Ralph C. Smedley
Founder

Table of Contents

Personally Speaking

The articles that Dr. Ralph C. Smedley wrote for The Toastmaster *magazine were written to members of Toastmasters Clubs. Invariably he wrote as though he were speaking personally to a man who was interested in what he had to say. He made no effort to argue his ideas; he explained them. To some extent this resulted in repetition but never contradiction. Nor was his reiteration more than is normal with a good teacher. On one occasion he wrote:*

When our Executive Director asked me for a special message for the 40th anniversary issue of THE TOASTMASTER, it reminded me of the minister who was asked if it wasn't about time for him to prepare a new sermon instead of harping on the same old subject every week. The minister replied, "I have several new sermons but I don't think I will give them until the congregation uses the old one first."

I would like to remind you of some of the principles that have helped us reach our 40th anniversary and to suggest that if we continue to practice them they will help us to reach our 60th, at least.

1. *Let's "keep it simple."* Our Basic Training program presents the fundamental principles of public speaking. These are the eternal verities of effective oral communication. Quintilian and Aristotle recognized them. Many men have written about public speaking in the intervening centuries, but they have not changed the simple basic principles, nor have they added very much to them.

2. *Toastmasters is a "do-it-yourself" activity.* We don't have an instruction manual for everything you do or say in your club. Nor should we have such manuals. Don't be afraid to use your imagination and initiative. Our motto encourages better listening and better thinking because these habits result in better speaking. Nobody can listen for you and nobody can do your thinking for you. Listen to others and evaluate their thinking—then form your own conclusions and speak for yourself.

3. *Toastmasters is based on belief in the individual*—and his ability to improve himself by developing to the fullest those abilities God has given him. Many organizations ask the individual to subordinate himself to the group. Ours is the only organization I know that is dedicated to the individual. We work together to bring out the best in each of us and then we apply our skills to help others.

4. Let us never forget that *we learn in moments of enjoyment*. Fellowship is important in Toastmasters. Our members stay in their clubs because they like each other and they are learning together.

If you observe these principles, I won't need to prepare a new message. Toastmasters will serve men for years to come!

This appeared in the 40th Anniversary issue of The Toastmaster, *October, 1964. For this occasion there was overt world-wide recognition of the contribution which Dr. Smedley had made through the Toastmasters organization. Among the messages he received was one from United States President Lyndon B. Johnson saying, "I congratulate you—and I commend you because you share the abiding faith of our government in the worth and dignity of every man."*

The Toastmasters Club

Probably the most comprehensive description of the concept of the Toastmasters Club and the philosophy of the Founder was made on his eightieth birthday (February 22, 1957):

THE TOASTMASTERS CLUB...
ITS MEANING AND VALUES

My conception of the Toastmasters Club, and of the training which it affords, while based on certain fundamental principles of education, is quite largely the result of experiences and observations through the past fifty years, when those principles have been put into practical use.

Our work is based primarily on the principles of learning by doing and improving through practice and criticism,—principles in which I strongly believe. Back of these, there is Herbert Spencer's definition of education. He held that education is a process of drawing out and putting into use the talents and abilities which are present in the person to be educated, rather than of pouring into his mind information from the exterior.

Added to these basic concepts is my conviction that the power to communicate is one of man's greatest endowments. I believe that all civilized life grows out of that ability, and the uses made of it. I believe that the improvement of man's ability to communicate his ideas is a means of improving life in all its phases, and that the progress of civilization depends on this improvement.

It was the very evident need for practical help in the art of communication which led me to organize the Toastmasters Club in the first place. Men in my community needed this aid, and they were glad to accept it when it was offered in an attractive and practical manner. The beginning was to meet a local need. There was no vision of future growth into a great organization.

My belief in the principles of learning by doing and improving through criticism led to the use of the methods which have served through all the years in the work of the Toastmasters Clubs.

The Toastmasters Club, as I see it, is a voluntary association of men who desire to gain facility in the art of communication.

These men can be encouraged to develop and use their own initiative and originality for their own improvement. It has been my privilege to share with all of them the results of my own experiences, and to try to stimulate them in using their resources.

It has been my conviction that formal courses should not be

offered in the Toastmasters Club, but I have been compelled to prepare certain materials which our members classify as "courses," in order to give guidance which was apparently needed. It appears to me to be desirable that the members should work out their problems, and then exchange their experiences, helping each other by pointing out better ways, as well as warning against ways which have not been found successful.

This is the course which we have followed as we have grown, and as men have asked for definite guidance. It has been my purpose to offer suggestions, leaving the application of these suggestions to the men, who will carry on in the manner best suited to their needs.

In the course of years, as we gained experience, it was seen that our processes had values far beyond the mere training of men to face audiences and speak their ideas. Communication was seen to have its effects in almost every phase of life. Improvement was needed not only in public speaking, but in all use of words, whether spoken or written. Training in speech had definite values in many lines of improvement. Some of these may be listed thus:

> It leads to the discovery of hidden abilities, bringing these latent talents into use, and thus enriching the man's life.
>
> It broadens the man's conception of how to live with people.
>
> It helps in the integration of personality.
>
> It brings out for use the leadership traits and abilities, and thus helps to prepare the man to be a leader.
>
> It opens the way to more creative and constructive living for the man who takes full advantage of the opportunities offered.

Thus our work has led us into fields of service far beyond the obvious task of training men for public speaking. Our responsibilities have been increased as we realized our task of opening the larger fields to those who come into membership.

Not every man follows through to gain the additional benefits. Not every club operates so as to give its members the most effective service. We fall short of the ideal of perfection, but we know that the individual member or the individual club has been helped, in proportion as the vision of possible accomplishment has been made clear, provided that the strong purpose has been present, either in the member or the club.

Men who have developed ability in leadership through working and serving as officers in their own clubs have gone on to wider fields of service in area and district affairs, and those who have exerted themselves to serve well have gained much in these enlarged fields of experience. Some few have gone on to the directorship of Toastmasters International, in which they have made personal gains in proportion to their willingness to learn. All have been helped to meet opportunities for leadership in their business or professional affairs, and in work for other organizations.

In common with many other agencies designed to help men, the Toastmasters Club is limited by the purpose of its members and by the sincerity of their desire for self-improvement. I know of no method whereby we can overcome the reluctance of men to think and plan and work to a purpose.

It may be said that most of our members come into a club to achieve some definite purpose. That purpose may be to learn to speak in public, to overcome fear, to gain skill in conducting a meeting, or to be a contest winner; or it may be any one of many purposes. It is our obligation to help them to adopt the best purpose, and then to work to accomplish.

When this immediate purpose has been achieved, the man is likely to drop out, unless the leadership of the club has been so good that he has been awakened to a realization of the further possibilities for him. No doubt this is the simple explanation for much of the turn-over in membership.

It appears to me that the obligation of the leaders of the movement, both those in the Board of Directors and those in the Home Office, is to offer supervision, explanation, suggestions, advice and inspiration wherever needed or desired, and to cooperate with local leaders so that our purposes may be fulfilled, in the helping of every member of every club to gain what he needs.

Training for this task is indispensable, and such training must proceed from those who are experienced to those lacking experience. Such help should be given in a cooperative spirit and manner, not so much by prescribed rules as by helpful suggestion.

At San Diego, in 1951, I stated:

"Education is our business. It has been so from the beginning. I do not know just why or how I happened to hit upon the idea that adult education could be handled in a social atmosphere, entirely apart from the formal classroom and standard academic procedure, but in some way I got that notion, and I have lived to see it not only recognized, but actually used, in circles where it was frowned upon a generation ago. There was evident agreement in my mind with the thought which Shakespeare had expressed long before when he caused one of his characters to say: 'No

16

profit grows where is no pleasure taken."

To my way of thinking, the Toastmasters Club is a very simple and practical use of the principles of education, applied to the helping of men in the effort to improve their capacity for living and wise enjoyment of life.

Simplicity has always been a characteristic of the club operation; and it should characterize all the work of the organization, from the higher executives through regions and districts and areas, always with the clear purpose of helping the local club to help its individual members.

Personal contacts between those who are prepared to lead and those who need help in leadership are essential. Much information must be transmitted through the printed page, but the most effective method of transmission is through training sessions in which qualified leaders present information and conduct discussion.

If we should ever lose this sense of fellowship, of personal, friendly relationships, we might easily become just another high-grade correspondence school. The personal touch, in all levels of our work, is one of its distinguishing features. We are working together.

I still hold to my opinion that we should not prescribe "courses," but should make the principles and ideals clear to all, permitting the men to deal with their own problems and to use their own resources so far as possible. It is our task to set up goals and standards and processes, which we can recommend to our clubs for use.

Fundamentally, I believe that the ability to communicate is a God-given talent, which ought to be used by all for the good of all. It is our privilege to help bring this talent into greater usefulness, so that it may be applied to the building of a better world, through the building of a better society made up of individuals who must act in groups. I believe that in bringing improvement in the way of "better thinking, better listening, better speaking" to individuals, we are contributing to the improvement of the society which is made up of these individuals.

I like the way that Orison S. Marden phrased his conception of speech training, when he wrote: "The ability to talk well is to a man what cutting and polishing are to the rough diamond. The grinding does not add anything to the diamond. It merely reveals its wealth."

(Feb. 1958, pp. 6-9)

Membership

Dr. Smedley only occasionally wrote about membership and the need for clubs to keep a full roster; no more than five percent of his writings deal with this problem. He was, of course, vitally concerned with the club program because he felt this determined the success of any group. Two brief articles provide a definitive statement of his attitude about membership as a club need.

Let us, during the next six months, increase the membership of each Toastmasters Club by at least five members. That seems simple, doesn't it? It can be done by improving the work in the club, and by letting people know of the work we are doing to help men.

But if we will do this, it will mean the addition of more than 17,000 men to our total membership, and that is the equivalent, in numbers, of organizing more than 500 new clubs. Think of establishing more than 500 new clubs in one year! Fantastic, isn't it? We would count that a world-beating achievement. But it can be done, by a reasonable effort on the part of each club, and in my opinion, it would be a far greater service to increase our membership in this manner, than to organize a thousand new clubs.

It is not a matter of increasing the size of Toastmasters, as an organization, but rather of making our training available to a greater number of men. To add five more members to your club should not be difficult, if your club is doing the kind of work in training men for communication which it should be doing. But the enlisting of these recruits can mean much to the world in which we live.

The nation needs our services, and so does the whole world. Through better communication, we can help to create better understanding, and understanding is what this world needs. Toastmasters International can be a powerful force for the improvement of world conditions.

A good many of our Toastmasters Clubs are working along with less than 20 active members. It is my opinion, based on long experience, that it is hardly possible for a club to operate successfully with less than 20 men in its activity. I wish that this challenge which I offer might raise the membership so that no Toastmasters Club would have less than this number, and so that a majority of our clubs would be operating with a minimum of 30 members.

Here we are, with a tremendous opportunity before us. It is a goal which can be reached and passed, if we put some thought and work into the task of bringing it to pass. And so I challenge you to get to work to bring our service up to this higher level of service. Let us share with others the benefits we have gained for ourselves.

(Oct. 1962, p. 12)

TRAINING IS PROGRESSIVE

A good club provides progressive speech training for older more experienced members. It gives them opportunity for longer, more formal and more advanced speeches. It gives them criticism adapted to their experience.

Can you imagine anything sillier than for a member of five or ten years standing to be given the same sort of elementary, kindergarten evaluation which serves for the beginner? The experienced man needs and should receive criticism appropriate to his experience and his ability to take it.

A good club uses experienced members for the coaching and training of new members. It gives them a chance to use their experience in connection with the Speechcraft Course, and the educational talks. It helps them locate outside speech appointments where they gain practice before strange and larger groups. It uses the old members.

LOSSES CAN BE MINIMIZED

Even the best Toastmasters Club, with the Educational Committee functioning at high efficiency, will lose some members, but these losses will be negligible compared to the losses in a club where the requirements of planned, progressive, coordinated training are overlooked.

If your club has suffered losses and a discouraging turnover in membership, or if attendance becomes a problem, do not too hastily scold the members. Turn the searchlight on the club's leadership, on their plans for training the members, on their educational aspirations, and on the ordinary programs at the regular meetings. The chances are that you will find right here the reason for the club's troubles, with the indicated solution of the problem.

The Toastmasters Club which has the right sort of program does not lose its members. The club whose membership is shrinking has something the matter with it.

(Oct. 1946, p. 17)

SPEECH IS A MEANS—NOT AN END

The statement of the subject is rather dogmatic. It may open the way to argument. We could spend some time on definitions or on a philosophical discussion of purposes and of volition in general. But we shall get further if we confine ourselves to discussion of the plain and practical issues involved, which may be bluntly stated. Why did you join a Toastmasters Club?

If it were possible to take a poll of our members, it is safe to assume that four out of five of them would say that they came into Toastmasters for speech improvement. Is there anything wrong in that?

Training in speech is the obvious purpose, the motivation of our clubs. It is something tangible, like the foothill you must climb before you start to ascend the high mountain. Certainly it is a means; in some cases, short-sighted people mistake the means for the end.

Just what do we mean by "means?"

It is the method or procedure by which we work toward some purpose. It is part of the foundation on which our enterprise is built.

Consider the child learning the alphabet, or the multiplication table. It is a real achievement when the youngster becomes able to recite the A-B-C's from A to Z, but if he stopped there, his accomplishment would be meaningless. He learns the alphabet in order that he may learn to read and write. If he stops short of that goal, he does not get far.

If we were to continue our polling of this audience, we would find that while all, or most of us, joined up for training in speech, most of us have gained far more than just the ability to make speeches. We have found speech training to be a means, or an instrumentality, by which we have made great pains—unforeseen gains—in our capacity to live and serve. Some of these unexpected gains have proved to be more valuable than the speech ability which was the primary incentive. Each step we have taken has brought us in sight of other steps which would not have been in our reach without the preliminary work, the means by which we have climbed.

In the Toastmasters Club, as in all other worthy enterprises, we find that progress leads to further progress. Understanding leads to the revealing of new ideas to be understood and used.

Men join our clubs for a variety of purposes, all of which are related to public speaking. One man joins to prepare himself to become president of his lodge or his service club. Another comes in to find how to overcome his self-consciousness and his inability to deal with other people.

We have seen a man come into our club whose self-consciousness was an affliction—almost a mental disease. He could not talk comfortably to anyone. He was afraid to meet people. He could not communicate intelligently. His fear of other people was an obsession. His lalophobia, or fear of speaking, had literally become a phobophobia, or fear of being afraid. He was just scared when he was with others, and he was handicapped by his fears.

We have seen this man develop, in the friendly, helpful atmosphere of his club, so that he could feel at ease in meeting and talking with other people. Thus he had accomplished the end for which he joined us. But he did not stop there. We have seen him discovering unsuspected abilities and bringing them into use, a new man in his personality, taking a new place in his community, and making amazing contributions to his environment. Speech was a means to this end, but accomplishment of his first purpose opened up so many new avenues for improvement that life took on a new aspect for him. He has not yet reached an end.

Perhaps we shall not be taking in too much territory if we say that the speech training, the training which is available in the Toastmasters Club, has values both psychological and pathological in addition to the obvious advantages which come with improvement in communication. Some of these values are coming to be recognized. Others are yet in the stages of discovery and exploration.

In the final analysis, although many men do not realize it, the end of our training is better communication. In the process of learning to communicate better, we get the other benefits, which come as extra dividends. As we gain speech facility, we gain in our thinking and in our listening powers. We extend our horizons and enlarge our interests. We become better neighbors. We help in the cause of human progress.

All civilization, all progress, depends on communication of ideas. As we learn to share our thoughts with others, and compare our own thinking with theirs, we make possible that cooperative action without which there can be no progress. We promote better understanding, on which human relations are based.

Thus we see that while most of us may have entered Toastmasters to learn to make speeches, that benefit is but the beginning of the good which may come to us, and the good which we may do for mankind.

(Feb. 1955, pp. 21-26)

Club Programs

The program of the Toastmasters Club was always of major importance to Dr. Smedley. Although he would seldom be so forthright as to say, "Now do this," or "This is the way your club should operate," he wrote frequently in manners to suggest specific ideas. Perhaps ten percent of his writing in The Toastmaster *related to club operation.*

I have been interested in the number of comments resulting from my quotation, at the Pittsburgh Convention, of my favorite saying about the Toastmasters Clubs. I have used it so often that I thought it was generally known. That quotation is, "We learn in moments of enjoyment." This seems to me to describe very adequately the theory and practice of Toastmasters.

The simple fact is that we grow or learn or work better when we enjoy what we are doing, and this is essentially the secret of success in Toastmasters. Our meetings are made enjoyable by a fine, helpful fellowship, in a pleasant social atmosphere, with activities carefully planned to give us profit "in moments of enjoyment."

This is why I am so insistent on program planning, so that there may be material presented which informs and inspires while it entertains.

Does your club measure up to this standard? If it does not, then you are advised to get to work to make its meetings the most attractive spot in town for the members when the hour of assembly comes around.

PROFIT AND PLEASURE

The program presented at the regular meeting is the key, the touchstone, the mainspring, of the club's progress and success.

The program is the laboratory process, the educational method, the training school, the stock in trade of the Toastmasters Club. Since it is so important, it should be given primary attention.

Every program must be planned. That has a familiar sound, does it not? Good programs result from study and conference and serious preparation. But the work pays off.

Every program must have a purpose. It is more than just giving a few members a chance to sound off. As a speech must be directed to the accomplishment of a definite purpose, so the entire program must lead to something specific, so that the member leaving the meeting can carry away with him the sense of something learned, something accomplished in this program.

Many of our clubs are weak in their program planning, which is the cause of low membership and unsatisfactory attendance, but it appears also that most of the clubs are weak in their work of evaluation. They recognize the weakness, but do not do much about it. Probably the reason is that skill in evaluation requires work—study and preparation—just the same as skill in speaking, and most of us are allergic to work.

(Nov. 1958, pp. 26-27)

SOME GOOD PROGRAMS

Some of our clubs—many of them, in fact—do plan excellent programs. For example, a club in Texas recently announced a program full of interesting subjects on the general theme of "How To." Here are the titles: How to Take Good Pictures; How to Prepare Your Car for Vacation; How to Have a Beautiful Yard; How to Plan Your Vacation; How to Live Comfortably in a Texas Summer.

A club in California devotes an evening to its own city. There are talks on: Our Parks; Our Fire Departments; Our City Hall; Our Traffic Problems; Our Tourist Attractions. You can add almost indefinitely to that list and be sure of a program of interest to every member. It might even lead to a newspaper story.

There is hardly any limit to the number of theme programs you can devise with a little use of the brain cells. Here is another list of subjects built around an imaginary tour of London and other parts of England:

The Tower of London; Hyde Park; The Houses of Parliament; London Bridge; Big Ben; Stratford on Avon; Westminster Abbey.

USE THE TABLE TOPICS

Table Topics cooked up on the spur of the moment can be largely a waste of time. When carefully planned, it becomes one of the most valuable parts of the training.

The training in impromptu speaking is valuable beyond our imagination, provided we use it right. Try making the club into a "town meeting" during the Topics period some evening. Propose some questions of local interest, and let the members engage in controversy to their hearts' content.

Never let it be forgotten that the Table Topics Master gets a wonderful chance for experience in presiding. His is a high privilege.

IN THE GOOD OLD SUMMERTIME

The meetings during the summer season need present no problem of attendance if your club puts on the right kind of programs. Make these programs so attractive and so full of interest that no man will miss one if he can help it. Good programs will help maintain good attendance and good interest. Let's try it this summer.

(June 1959, pp. 28-29)

YOUR CLUB'S HISTORY

Every organization of a permanent nature should keep a record of its history, showing its important activities, its officers, its members, and other information which may be useful from time to time. Every Toastmasters Club should keep such a record.

This record may be made a responsibility of the secretary, both as to keeping it up to date and as to preserving it safely for posterity; or it may be a task committed to some member appointed for that special task. In any case, it should not be overlooked nor neglected.

It is not an infrequent occurrence for some club officer to write to the Home Office asking for the date of chartering of his club, or for a list of the charter members, or for a copy of the club's bylaws. Apparently his club has not preserved any such vital records. Our records of the individual clubs are sufficient to furnish the answers to many of the questions, but there are others on which we have no information. The club itself should have the records from its beginning, whether in minute books, the club bulletin, or some other form.

We recommend that each Toastmasters Club undertake to discover what historical information it has available, where it is kept and who is responsible for it. This may be a project for your club. Investigate, and see what procedure is needed. The present can always learn from experiences of the past, and today's activities may be an aid to men in days yet to come, if properly recorded.

THE ICE BREAKER

This is the subject for the first project in our Basic Training Manual. It is assigned so as to help the novice by letting him talk about a subject on which he is well informed—himself and his life— but it has values far beyond making it easier for the beginner.

The Ice Breaker introduces the man to his fellows. It lets them know something about what kind of person he is, where he came from, why he is here, and whither he is heading. After hearing the brief story of his background, the other men are in a better position to help him with their evaluations and suggestions for improvement.

But the biographical, personal speech is not limited in value to this one presentation. It would be fine practice for each Toastmaster to give a talk about himself once every year. I suggest that you try it.

Suppose you have been a member for a year, or for two or three or a dozen years. There is much about you, your occupation, your thinking, which the other men do not know. It will help them to help you if they know some of these facts, and it will be good for you to arrange the information to present to them.

We are all interested in becoming better acquainted with our fellow men. That is why the introductory speech is heard with so much interest. We can promote better friendship and understanding in our club by occasional presentation of the self-centered subject. The better we know each other, the more intelligently we can help. Revive and review the autobiographical Ice Breaker occasionally in your program, and see what good results it will bring.

BE A CRUSADER

We miss a great opportunity through failure to present subjects of importance, on which we have deep convictions. We speak best when we are in earnest, and by presenting our convictions we stimulate others to think and act.

The Toastmasters Club has a definite function as a sort of "town meeting" in which ideas are exchanged on matters of current interest. This function is fulfilled when programs are planned to that end, and when speakers are assigned to discuss the subjects which need consideration.

One of the most immediately important subjects before the public today is the menace of communism to our institutions of freedom. This is a subject on which the general public is not well informed. It presents itself to every Toastmasters Club with a challenge to study and formulate opinions which will result in needed action.

I recommend to every Toastmaster the recently published book by J. Edgar Hoover, entitled "Masters of Deceit," which presents a factual study, based on long experience, of this ideology which is working itself so insidiously into American life, threatening the extinction of our cherished ideals and institutions. Any man of intelligence will be stirred by this book as he reads it, and he will be impelled to discuss it with others. And this is true of men of all free nations.

Let us, as good citizens, seek to inform ourselves, and then speak and act. "Be in earnest" is a good theme for every speaker. Here is a subject on which you can really be in earnest. Try it. Your club is a good starting place.

(July 1959, pp. 28-29)

YOUR CLUB IS—A LABORATORY

A laboratory, originally, is the workroom of the chemist. By extension in use, it has come to signify any place where some operation is performed. In that sense, a Toastmasters Club is properly called a laboratory, for it is a place where many experiments are tried, and many operations are tested.

Every member, if he is awake to his opportunity, uses his club as his personal laboratory in speech. Even though he is not definitely conscious of doing so, he tries out different methods of delivery, various methods of selecting speech subjects and arranging his materials. He discovers which methods produce best results, and then he experiments further for the improvement of his use of these methods.

Not only in the making of speeches does he get the chance to work by trial and error methods. He tries different ways of listening and evaluating, for every member, if he is wise, evaluates for himself every speech which he hears.

There are opportunities to try out various applications of speech, such as may occur in daily work.

The salesman may use his club for the try-out of some selling technique. The teacher may experiment with some teaching method which can be applied later in the classroom. The purchasing agent or the personnel director may try some of his procedures before the club, and profit by the evaluation which he receives.

Perhaps a member is asked to make speeches for the Red Cross or the March of Dimes or the Community Chest, or in behalf of the proposed bond issue to build more schools. Here in his club is a ready-made audience, prepared to listen analytically and to point out ways by which he can improve his presentation.

A Toastmaster who had charge of a machine shop employing many men gave a demonstration speech showing how he instructed a new employee. He found, through the observations of his evaluators, that he muddled things up by his explanation rather than making them clear. After two or three attempts before the club, he was able to report a definite improvement in production from his department, simply because he had learned how to give explanations and instructions in an understandable fashion.

An optician, called upon to deliver an important address at a state convention of men of his profession, practiced on his club with mutual profit. He was shown how to present his subject more effectively, and the men who listened to him learned many useful facts about the care of their eyes.

A member who was seeking a new position gave a sample talk in which he tried to sell himself and his abilities to the prospective employer. The result was a vast improvement in his presentation, and finally, a successful interview with the man for whom he hoped to work.

A man whose speech was desperately boring because of his monotonous manner of talking deliberately set about doing things which he considered ridiculous as he spoke to the club. He yelled and roared and used numerous devices to break his bad habit, and he broke it, largely by finding out that some of the actions which had seemed ridiculous proved to be very good procedure, when kept under control.

This man, like many another Toastmaster, discovered that his Toastmasters Club was a place where a man can act the fool without really being foolish.

All speech is for communication, and there is no possibility of communication unless people understand. Your club can help you to find out whether you are making yourself understood.

Take some business letter which you have written, and read it to the club, asking for comments. Ask them if it made the sale or answered the question or created better relations. Ask them how it could be better stated. Out of the reactions you will get valuable suggestions.

Discuss the display advertisement which you have laid out and ask how to make it better. They will tell you.

Your Toastmasters Club is your laboratory in which to try experiments in better communication. You can try anything once before this frank but sympathetic audience, and you can learn by listening to their comments.

Approach your experiments with an honest and open mind, seeking improvement rather than confirmation of your preconceived notions, and your laboratory will bring you to new accomplishments, new discoveries, new inventions, which may mean new and desirable advancement to you.

(June 1955, pp. 13-14)

Club Leadership

The development of effective club programs and the maintenance of a dynamic group in each club inevitably required leadership. Dr. Smedley wisely directed considerable attention to the responsibilities as well as the opportunities available to the officers. Here are two articles twenty years apart which stress these points.

NEW OFFICERS

Many men will be stepping into office in their clubs this month. It is to be hoped that every one of them will realize the opportunity placed before him in this new responsibility, and that none of them will fail to make use of his privilege to serve.

For the club officer, the opportunity is twofold. First, he assumes responsibility for the progress and welfare of his club. Whatever his position may be, it carries obligations on matters essential to the successful operation of the organization. Whether the officer is president or secretary or sergeant at arms, or vice president, his duties are clearly specified in the bylaws and in the various guides on club operation, and it is his business to know and understand these duties.

Second, he steps into a phase of leadership which can be of great value in his own personal development. Being an officer may involve extra service in the performance of his tasks, but it opens the way to new growth and development in his own life. There are rewards for him, if he will claim them. He will grow through the experiences he encounters in the work which his office involves.

(March 1964, p. 12)

WHEN YOU PRESIDE

Many newly elected presidents of clubs are gaining their first experiences as presiding officers at this time. Not only for the good of the club, but also for the good and the advancement of the official himself, he needs to make the most of his office. An efficient president can save time and expedite work, just as a careless or inefficient one can waste time and wear out his fellow members.

When you preside, it is your duty to know the business which is to come before the meeting and the allotment of time. You have a schedule, carefully timed, prepared before the meeting and you are ready to put it through on time.

A meeting is properly opened by use of the gavel. Make sure that one is provided. Don't depend on rattling a spoon against a glass, or clearing your throat. Have a gavel and use it. Rap sharply once or twice. Do not give a series of hesitating, indecisive taps. Start with decision. Make the opening sharp, clear and authoritative by correct use of the gavel.

When you preside, remember that you are in charge of the business of the meeting. Unless you call someone else to take the chair in your place, it is your responsibility to handle all matters requiring action. You may introduce a program chairman or a toast-master to present a program, but if any matter of business arises in the course of the program which requires formal action, you, as president, take over control for the time being. You are not a dictator, nor the operator of a steam-roller, but you are the responsible head of the organization and its business is your business.

When you preside, avoid set formulas for dealing with recurring situations. In introducing a program chairman or other chairman, do not make it a rule always to "turn over a meeting." Use less violent methods. Vary the formula. You can yield the gavel to him, or surrender control, or ask him to take charge. Better still, you can introduce him cleverly, just as you would a speaker or an entertainer and say nothing about yielding or turning over.

When you come to the end of the meeting, once more avoid a set formula. In a session which has been run by the program schedule and for which the time of adjournment has been fixed in advance, you do not need to ask for a motion to adjourn. Similarly, you do not really need to ask, "Is there anything else to come before us?"

If there is anything else to come up, you, as president, ought to know of it. Do not become a slave to the habit of saying, "If there is nothing else to come up, the meeting is adjourned." Find other and better ways to say it. For example, you might try, "This concludes the evening's program and the meeting is adjourned." Or you can speak a complimentary word to the program chairman or committee and announce adjournment. It can be done in many different phrases. Don't overdo any one form. Seek variety.

When you preside, keep one eye on the clock. If the meeting is well planned, there is a definite time to start and to stop. Do not disregard either. Start promptly, if it is humanly possible. When the closing time arrives, do not let the meeting run over except by approval of the audience.

As presiding officer, be on your toes all the time. Let every word you speak be given clearly and carefully. Take advantage of your opportunity to gain practice in making short speeches, all of them good. Be sure that you are prepared and then proceed to preside with confidence and certainty. People more willingly follow a leader who knows where he is going.

(May 1943, pp. 4-5)

TRAINING FOR LEADERSHIP

In 1954, the year of the thirtieth anniversary, Dr. Smedley moved more directly into the continuing controversy over what is leadership and in what manner does the Toastmasters Club aid in its development.

CAN LEADERSHIP BE TAUGHT?

That the world needs competent leaders is a statement not open to dispute. Where and how are these leaders to be found? That is another question.

A metropolitan daily recently headlined the account of a conference of educators with the words: "Colleges Urged to Teach Leadership." This raises still another question. Can leadership be taught? Can people be made into leaders through education?

There is no question that the principles of intellectual and personality training can be presented to students for assimilation, and that both knowledge and personality are essential elements in equipment for leadership; but unless the qualities which make for leadership are present in the individual, it is hardly possible that any amount of instruction will ever make him a leader. You can't train a man to be a painter or a pianist unless he has some natural ability. Neither can you teach leadership to people who lack leadership ability.

But just what do we mean by "leadership?" It would appear to be the capacity to look ahead, think ahead, plan ahead, and then influence other people to go ahead on the plan. Walter Lippmann wrote, "The final test of a leader is that he leaves behind him in other men the conviction and the will to carry on."

Some people are equipped by nature for such thinking and influencing. Some have the ability to study, evaluate, reason, foresee, and then to formulate plans to bring their visions into reality. More than that, they can inspire their associates to work for the same purposes. These are the natural leaders. Give them a reasonable amount of education and opportunity, and they will stand out from the crowd.

There are some who aspire to be leaders because they like to feel powerful. They want to order others around. They want their word to be law.

Often there is some youthful experience of frustration in the background for such as these, or perhaps some unfulfilled ambition. There is a definite self interest, a wish to be served rather than to serve.

This is the stuff of which dictators are made. Men of this stripe may develop into Napoleons or Hitlers. They make good followers of the authoritarian line. They want to lead for their own sakes, not for the good of society.

A real leader, cooperative rather than dictatorial, is altruistic in disposition. He has ideals which he believes may be good for others, and he tries to establish them because they are good, not because they will make him rich or powerful, or even make him feel better. He is not primarily concerned about his own glory or enrichment. He is willing to stay out of the spotlight, so long as he is helping his fellow men.

Experience has demonstrated that many men possess the capacity for leadership without realizing it. Their talents lie dormant for lack of the needed awakening. But unsuspected abilities may be revealed to a man on his job. He may seek further self-improvement through studies and special training. This is the way to discover and develop leaders, rather than to attempt to "teach leadership."

Self expression is one of the first steps toward leadership. When a man learns to express himself intelligently, he discovers that he has knowledge or experience which is of interest and value to others. This gives him a new sense of appreciation for himself.

At the same time, his associates discover in him depths of knowledge and talent which they had not suspected. This gives them a new appreciation for him, and for what he can do.

Unless other circumstances stand in the way, these discoveries lead to his being called upon to serve in activities which had been completely out of his reach before the awakening. Thus he may become a leader, to whatever extent his capacity will permit.

Leadership cannot be taught, but the qualities for leadership which are present in a man can be developed and revealed and made available for use through training in self-expression and self-control. Leaders can be taught and trained. Thus may be justified the idea of "leadership through speech," provided we realize that speechmaking in itself is not an end, but merely one step, and a very important one, in the direction of preparing for service and leadership.

To quote Lippmann once more: "The genius of a good leader is to leave behind him a situation which common sense, without the grace of genius, can deal with successfully."

But to be able to organize and establish such situations is a task which requires both genius and training, and training in communication is fundamental in preparation, a desideratum for every leader.

(Aug. 1954, pp. 3-4)

Parliamentary *Practice*

Within the leadership range came the emphasis on parliamentary procedure. Dr. Smedley approached the matter very practically as part of club conduct. He expressed both his respect for General Robert and his deep appreciation and understanding of the Rules of Order *in other publications including* The Amateur Chairman, *but in* The Toastmaster *Magazine he applied the rules and regulations both to leadership functioning and to club operation.*

THE PRESIDENT

The president of any assembly is the one, literally, who "sits out in front." That is the literal meaning of the word in its Latin background, *praesidere, (prae,* before, plus *sedere,* to sit.)

Other titles are applied to him, in accordance with the preference of the organization. He may be the chairman, in which case he occupies the chair in the meeting. Other members may sit in chairs also, but the chairman has the chair of office or of honor, from which he conducts the meeting.

In some assemblies he is known as the moderator. In this capacity he may be expected to serve as an arbitrator or umpire or controller, who guides and restrains.

Whatever his title may be, the president's duties are quite plain and simple. He serves primarily to keep things moving in orderly fashion, making decisions as to procedure and guiding the work so as to get the business done in a prompt and democratic manner. He is not a "boss" nor a dictator. He is primarily the servant of the organization. Tact and courtesy are his characteristics. To these he should add good judgment and an open mind.

Sometimes there appears to be an impression that the one chosen to be president is thereby miraculously endowed with almost infinite wisdom and power. When he becomes president, he may think that he has all knowledge and understanding, and his word is law. His will must not be thwarted. That is what he thinks. He will learn better, or he will have a miserable time.

Any person who takes the office with that notion in his mind is fore-doomed to disappointment and failure. If he is presiding over an assembly of plain speaking, clear thinking people who know their way about, he will find himself checked, corrected, and generally put in his place.

The duties of the president are quite lucidly set forth by Robert, in the "Rules." Here we find that his first business is to call the meeting to order at the appointed time, not half an hour late. He comes before the assembly with the order of business before him, and he announces the business to be considered in the order in which it is to be acted upon. If any special matters are to be considered, outside of the ordinary routine business, he will have at hand the agenda, which has been prepared in advance in conference with his Executive Committee or his Board of Directors. He recognizes speakers, states motions which are offered, conducts the discussion, and puts matters to a vote. After the voting, he announces the results.

When discussion is in progress, he restrains the members, keeping them within the established rules of order, and he enforces the observance of order and decorum. When questions of order arise, he makes the decision, always subject to an appeal.

He does not act as a dictator, and his rulings are not arbitrarily given, but are always based on the principles of right and justice, and on the accepted rules of procedure. The assembly may reject his rulings by a formal vote, in which case he gracefully accepts their decisions.

In general, he represents the assembly, and by his signature he authenticates the orders and proceedings which have been adopted. In all things, according to Robert, he obeys the commands of the meeting or the organization as expressed in its corporate actions.

As a matter of practice, the president is supposed to stand instead of sitting when he puts a motion to a vote, and when discussion is a matter of short remarks by various members who wish recognition. When a lengthy speech is being made, he takes his chair and relaxes. In smaller groups or in the case of informal meetings, he may sit or stand as he prefers, but he must always be in the position of control or direction.

The president is entitled to vote when the voting is by ballot, and in other cases when his vote will change the result, either by creating a tie or by breaking it. In case of a motion which refers especially to the president or chairman, the maker of the motion should put it to the vote, thus sparing the chairman the embarrassment of calling for a vote of thanks or censure for himself. In no case does the president have a right to cast more than one vote.

A wise president never takes advantage of his position to enter into a discussion. If he wishes to talk about the matter being debated, he calls another member, preferably the vice president, to take the chair for the time being, while he, the president, secures the floor and speaks on the level with the other members. He does not assume the chairmanship again until the matter under discussion has been disposed of by vote.

The president, then, needs to realize the nature of his position, which is that of a guide, an umpire, and a leader; never a dictator nor an arbitrary ruler. He develops plans, in consultation with his fellow officers, and he proposes what he believes to be wise action, but he is always more concerned about securing thoughtful and unanimous action by those over whom he presides than he is about getting his own way.

Tact, open-mindedness and courteous consideration for the opinions of others are characteristic of the good chairman.

Robert states a definite opinion in these words: "The presiding officer of a large assembly should never be chosen for any reason except his ability to preside."

This opinion will find many dissenters in ordinary practice, for there are, quite obviously, other essential qualifications; but the ability to preside impartially, courteously and intelligently is essential to successful chairmanship.

The opportunity to serve as president or chairman is something to be desired by any ambitious man who is willing to be of service. It is an experience calculated to reveal and develop latent characteristics of leadership, and to broaden the scope of life for the man who serves well.

The man who seeks the position for purposes of self-gratification and personal glory is headed for trouble and disappointment. The ideal president is the one who realizes that, while he "sits out in front" or leads the forward march of his organization, he is still "servant of all."

(Jan. 1955, pp. 1-2 & 26)

PARLIAMENTARY PRACTICE FOR ALL

When we speak of parliamentary practice, we usually associate it with the duties of the chairman or president, but that is not nearly a wide enough application. Every member of an assembly needs to have at least some understanding of procedures in order to be an intelligent participant.

Even the best informed and most experienced presiding officer can be hampered in the performance of his duties by situations created by the ignorance of members of the group over which he presides. When this ignorance is intensified by an ambition to be heard and observed, the problems really become bad.

The unversed member offers motions which are out of order, or questions the propriety of motions which are entirely in order, or he interrupts debate on a question by introducing extraneous matter, or he proceeds in various other ways to throw the meeting off the track, simply because he does not understand how business is properly carried on.

Parliamentary practice in the club is essential, not only to give members experience in presiding, but still more important, to train them in participation. For this reason, it is especially important that all such practice efforts be carefully planned, so as to demonstrate the right methods and avoid confusion. Some clubs have made the mistake of turning parliamentary practice into disorderly, more or less ridiculous exhibitions, the net result of which is to add to the confusion in the minds of the participants.

It is a very wise plan to devote the table topics period of the club meeting to parliamentary training, once a month. With well-planned projects carried through in orderly manner, the members can gain much good from such a policy.

(Aug. 1959, p. 24)

Speechmaking

As would be expected, a large proportion of the writing that Dr. Smedley published in The Toastmaster magazine was devoted to speechmaking and evaluation. Probably half of his contributions were devoted to these phases of the Toastmasters educational program.

Dr. Smedley related Toastmasters and their work to many of the classical and later famous speakers and teachers of speech including Cicero, Demosthenes, Patrick Henry, Henry Clay, Henry Grady and others whose influences are known through history. Typical of these discussions was this article on the importance of Quintilian as an example for Toastmasters. Dr. Smedley's understanding of the history and criticism of public address gives him a status as a scholar in the area, a fact which he too readily allowed to remain unrecognized.

AN OLD ROMAN SPEAKS

The modern student of speech ought to know the works of Marcus Fabius Quintilian, whose teachings on the art of public speaking are as modern as tomorrow morning's newspaper and as helpful as your favorite critic in the Toastmasters Club meeting. Unfortunately, Quintilian's monumental work, "Institutes of Oratory," is not easily accessible. The translation by the Rev. John Selby Watson, published in 1885 as part of the Bohn Classical Library, is found generally only in the more extensive libraries.

First, who was Quintilian?

He was a Roman, born in Spain about 40 A.D. Educated in Rome as a youth, he won distinction in the two professions of pleader and teacher of speech. Pliny the Younger seems to have been one of his pupils. For years he was a familiar figure in the Roman courts, but eventually he retired and spent still further years in composing his work on speech, embodying the results of a lifetime of study and observation. He seems to have been impelled to do this because some of his pupils had published their notes on his lectures as a textbook, under his name. In order to correct the false impressions given by the work of these misguided enthusiasts, he undertook to write his own story, for which we are greatly indebted to him.

His book was lost to human view for centuries after the fall of Rome. In the early days of the revival of learning Poggio the Florentine found a manuscript of the "Institutes" in the monastery of St. Gall, near Constance, and made a transcript from it with his own hand. A letter written by this ancient indicates the date of his discovery as 1417. This manuscript is supposed to be the one which is now preserved at Florence under the name of the *Codex Laurentianus.*

Here we offer selected paragraphs from the first chapters of the "Institutes." These have been chosen as being representative of the thought and method of the teacher.

From the preface: "We are to form, then, the perfect orator, who cannot exist unless as a good man; and we require of him, therefore, not only consummate ability in speaking, but every excellence of mind. For I cannot admit that the principles of moral and honorable conduct are, as some have thought, to be left to the philosophers; since the man who can duly sustain his character as a citizen, who is qualified for the management of public and private affairs, and who would govern communities by his counsels, settles them by means of laws, and improves them by judicial enactments, can certainly be nothing else but an orator.

"Let the orator, therefore, be such a man as may be called truly wise, not blameless in morals only (for that, in my opinion, though some disagree with me, is not enough) but accomplished also in science, and in every qualification for speaking; a character such as, to aim at perfection, for which most of the ancients strove; who, though they thought that no wise man had yet been found, nevertheless laid down directions for gaining wisdom.

"It is to be stated, however, in the first place, that precepts and treatises on art are of no avail without the assistance of nature; and these instructions, therefore, are not written for him to whom talent is wanting, any more than treatises on agriculture for barren ground.

"There are also certain other natural aids, as power of voice, a constitution capable of labor, health, courage, gracefulness; qualities which, if they fall to our lot in a moderate degree, may be improved by practice, but which are often so far wanting that their deficiency renders abortive the benefits of understanding and study; and these very qualities likewise are of no profit in themselves without a skillful teacher, persevering study and great and continued exercise in writing, reading and speaking."

Quintilian maintains that the education of an orator dates from infancy. His thought is that the earliest training of the child should lay the foundations for effective speech. Thus he advises that the nurse be selected with a proper attention to her ability in correct use of language. "Before all things, let the talk of the child's nurses not be ungrammatical...To their morals, doubtless, attention is first to be paid; but let them also speak with propriety. It is they that the child will hear first; it is their words that he will try to form of imitation

...Let the child not be accustomed, then, even while he is yet an infant, to phraseology which must be unlearned."

The author is insistent on the importance of study of grammar, the choice of words, and care in enunciation. Indeed, the earlier chapters of the work constitute an authoritative treatment of the theory and practice of grammar which applies to English as well as the Latin tongue. But Quintilian goes further, in demanding that the education of the orator be much broader than merely the study of speech. It must embrace music, art, science and all forms of knowledge, including mathematics.

"But geometry has a still greater connection with the art of oratory. Order, in the first place, is necessary in geometry; and is it not also necessary in eloquence? Geometry proves what follows from what precedes, what is unknown from what is known; and do we not draw similar conclusions in speaking? Does not the well known mode of deduction from a number of proposed questions consist almost wholly in syllogisms?"

Modern to the last word is the teaching as to pronunciation, enunciation and facial expression.

"What then, is the duty of the teacher?...Let him, in the first place, correct faults of pronunciation, if there be any, so that the words of the learner may be fully expressed, and that every letter may be uttered with its proper sound...The teacher will be cautious, likewise, that concluding syllables be not lost; that his pupil's speech be all of a similar character; that whenever he has to raise his voice, the effort may be that of his lungs and not of his head; that his gestures may be suited to his voice, and his looks to his gesture. He will have to take care, also, that the face of his pupil, while speaking, look straight forward; that his lips be not distorted; that no opening of the mouth immoderately distend his jaws; that his face be not turned up, or his eyes cast down too much, or his head inclined to either side. The face offends in various ways; I have seen many speakers, whose eyebrows were raised at every effort of the voice; those of others I have seen contracted; and those of some even disagreeing, as they turn up one towards the top of the head, while the other eye itself was almost concealed. To all these matters, as we shall hereafter show, a vast deal of importance is attached; for nothing can please which is unbecoming."

In that last sentence this great Roman enunciated a principle which no speaker can afford to disregard. Mannerisms of every sort must be evaluated on this basis. All our speech habits must be ruled by it. That which is unbecoming in our speech must be displeasing to our hearers. That which displeases does not win votes nor make sales. *"Nothing can please which is unbecoming."*

The speaker who will study with care the work of Quintilian will gain immeasurably in his ability in speech, and he will discover that the arts and problems of speech are not greatly changed today from what they were in Rome two thousands years ago.

(March 1939, pp. 10-12)

The Speaker and His Subject

One of the principal areas discussed by all who write about speaking relates to the speaker and his topic and subject-matter. This division is found from classical times to the most modern. Dr. Smedley considered the speaker as a man worthy of his audience, and was greatly concerned that Toastmasters not only present themselves well but that they talk on appropriate topics and be informed on all subjects they discussed. The first article presented below is subtle but certainly to the point. The other articles under this general heading are typical of his point of view.

TOASTMASTERS AS EDUCATORS

When we talk about what we get out of the Toastmasters Club, we speak freely of the value of practice in facing an audience, in learning to speak, in giving and receiving criticism, and in discovering and training our unsuspected abilities, but we usually overlook one benefit which seems to me to be worthy of special mention.

That benefit is the educational value of the speeches and discussions heard in the club meetings.

In the typical Toastmasters Club of 30 members, you will find from 10 to 15 different professions, businesses or lines of interest represented. Each member, as his turn comes to speak, presents ideas and information based on his individual experiences, and differing, for that reason, from those presented by others. The educational value of such speeches is worthy of emphasis, even if there were nothing further to be gained.

Suppose the club meets weekly, throughout the year. Allowing for a couple of meetings which may fall on holidays, the club will meet 50 times. On the average there will be 1000 or more impromptu talks given in the Table Topics discussions.

Suppose I am able to attend only 42 of the 50 meetings. On the other evenings I have to go to lodge meetings or to a church social, or take my family to the movies. But at the 42 meetings I attend I shall have the opportunity to listen to approximately 250 speeches on about as many topics, each presented by a speaker who has given study and thought to the subject.

If I can't derive some useful information from these speeches, I should have my head examined by a specialist. The club educates me.

For example, take the case of a good, typical Toastmasters Club in a typical American city. It numbers in its membership two doctors, a dentist, a realtor, three schoolteachers, two insurance men, a motor mechanic, an automobile salesman, a farmer, a building contractor, two merchants, two bankers, a minister, a newspaper man, a radio technician, and men of various other interests. With such diversity of material, the club programs are always distinguished for interest and variety of information.

If I had faithfully kept notes on the speeches in my own club, I would now possess a collection of data dealing with all sorts of matters, some of which would certainly come in handy, and all of which would add to my knowledge.

Right in this club I have heard talks on aviation, banking, credit, discoveries, education, foreign trade, gun powder, health insurance, ice manufacture, kodaks, local improvements, taxes, metallurgy, Olympic games, peace, quetzals, farm management, trout fishing, submarines, atomic warfare, and so on through the alphabet and back again.

I have listened to a debate on public ownership of utilities, a panel discussion on elimination of traffic hazards, and a symposium on crime and its cure.

In the course of listening to these scores of talks on as many subjects, I have picked up information, broadened my outlook, and corrected mistaken notions.

Perhaps I should not go quite so far as to say that I found a year in the Toastmasters Club equal in value to a course in college, but I can say emphatically that I did take two or three courses in college which gave me not half the educational help which I have gained in listening to the speeches of my fellow Toastmasters. All of this, of course, takes no account of what I gained through my own practice in preparing and delivering speeches, and in giving and taking criticism.

We Toastmasters make a great mistake when we fail to emphasize the informational and cultural value of our programs. Even if I never opened my mouth in our meetings except to take food, attendance would be worth while for what I would learn. Open ears would bring me full value for my investment.

To the other values of Toastmasters training let us add this one, with emphasis—that it is the busy man's best chance to take a post graduate course in general information without inconvenience or loss of time.

Toastmasters are educators, whether they realize it or not, and Toastmasters is more than a club—it's an education.

(Aug. 1950, pp. 13-14)

THE MAN WITH THE MESSAGE

People will listen to the man with a message, if he knows how to deliver it. With your training in Toastmasters, your delivery should be effective. Choose your subject, one on which you can develop real convictions; then inform yourself, and go to talking about it.

(Oct. 1956, pp. 7-8)

"DON'T DABBLE IN DIRT..."

When Harry W. Mattison was President of Toastmasters International, he gave us this motto, and even had it printed on cards for us to keep before us as a constant reminder. Apparently it is time to reprint the words, perhaps in larger type than before. The tendency towards the risqué, the off-color, the suggestive story, is always in evidence. The warning to "keep it clean" has to be sounded over and over again.

This article is such a warning. It is an attempt to present fairly and frankly the arguments against indecency.

Wilbur D. Nesbitt was a popular master of ceremonies and after-dinner speaker a generation ago. He had a keen sense of humor and a wonderful fund of good stories, and he was in demand as a banquet attraction. But he was notably careful in his choice of material. In his book, *"After-Dinner Speeches and How to Make Them,"* he explains his attitude in these words:

"Never use an off-color or suggestive story. It may make a hit when told, but the after-effect is bad. We invite people to speak to us because we respect them, and we want them to respect us. We, the audience, consider ourselves a pretty decent, respectable, upstanding lot of folks. When you tell a suggestive story to us, you intimate that you have decided that is our level. It may be—but we don't want it made a matter of public knowledge."

What Mr. Nesbitt has said here so tactfully is something that every right-minded man has realized many a time. You have had the experience, yourself. You were in a meeting where someone started off with stories which made you ashamed. Your problem was whether to remain and subject yourself to the flow of dirt, or to get up and walk out, at the risk of being counted a prude, or to forget your own ideals and join in laughter at things which were not funny—merely dirty. No speaker has a right to put his hearers into such a situation.

But why do people indulge in questionable humor—"dabble in dirt?"

There are several reasons—scientific, psychological reasons. Let's take a look at a few of them—the least embarrassing ones, if you please.

First, I mention immaturity of intellect. Much unclean humor used by men who have reached years of maturity is indicative of mental under-development, such as is shown by the small boy who writes naughty words on back fences. Use of the off-color joke is an evidence of an adolescent mind, a retarded mental growth, whatever the actual age of the perpetrator. In a word, it is childish.

Second, the habit is a characteristic of the exhibitionist. He wants to attract attention, perhaps applause. Conscious that his own thoughts are not of sufficient importance or interest to gain distinction, he resorts to dirt as a means to show off.

Third, it is evidence of limited mental capacity. It reflects lack of mental balance, such as should characterize the adult mind. It springs from deficiency of knowledge and culture, and from absence of good taste. The man who resorts to unclean humor advertises his own intellectual shortage.

But my strongest personal objection to the unclean in speech is based on the way it affects my dealing with men. There is a natural tendency in the human mind to remember stories and illustrations of a striking nature. A pointed story stays with you when the speech in which it was contained has faded from memory. And this is especially true of the off-color stories. They stick, like mud which dries on your clothing and leaves a permanent stain.

To my regret, I find that there are a good many people whom I remember through the years, not by the fine qualities which they must have possessed, or the good things they must have said, but by some vile story or saying which stays in my mind in spite of me. I don't like to remember people that way.

There are so many memories of that sort, memories of men whom I have really liked and admired, but whose place in my thought is marred by spots of dirt which cover up good things I would like to recall. For my part, I would hate to have anyone remember me by anything of that sort.

There is another argument against the use of the risqué, in the effect it has on the speaker. He finds himself in a situation where even he can realize that uncleanness is out of place, so he has to revise his speech before he can use it. Or he may have lost his sense of fitness, so that he goes ahead with something quite unacceptable, having become so accustomed to dirt that he does not realize what he is doing.

The world is so well stocked with keen, clean fun that there is no excuse for playing in the mud to get a laugh. You can write it down as an axiom that someone may be offended by an off-color joke, but that no person is likely to take offense at a clean one.

I am proud of the fact that smut is so rarely introduced into a Toastmasters Club meeting. Now and then some misguided speaker gets off the reservation, but he is certain to be called to time by some of the wiser ones. Thus we manage to keep fairly clean in a smutty world.

Use humor to illuminate your speech. Let your talks scintillate with wit. Make your stories appropriate, pointed, well spoken. Let them be windows to make the light shine on your argument. But keep it clean.

"Don't Dabble in Dirt!"

(July 1947, pp. 14-15)

BE CAREFUL WHAT YOU SAY...

You have freedom to speak as you will. But this freedom implies an obligation to speak carefully, thoughtfully, wisely. What you say carelessly may be taken seriously by people far beyond your own circle, with catastrophic results.

The world of today has grown small, and communications have become almost instantaneous. Isolation of thought, put into words, is no longer a possibility. Any word, once spoken, may take wings and fly to the uttermost parts of the earth.

Some inquirers are troubled by what they think is an indication that we have reversed our policy. The fact that the article was published in the magazine is interpreted by some to mean that it is an expression of change of attitude on the part of the organization.

This is not at all the case. The fact that an article appears in the magazine does not necessarily mean that it reflects a policy of Toastmasters. It expresses the ideas of the writer. He is entitled to his own opinions and beliefs.

I must reiterate the frequently repeated statement that Toastmasters International does not lay down rigid rules for its members or for all speakers to follow. We recommend such methods and policies as seem desirable, but every speaker is at liberty to think for himself and make his own choices.

But what about this "thank you" business? If Toastmaster Tully prefers to end his speech with a "thank you" that is his privilege. It is your privilege if you think that it adds to the effectiveness of your talking. In my opinion, the effect of a speech is weakened when the speaker gasps "thank you" as he subsides into his chair. Frequently it is an expression of nervousness or the admission that he has nothing more to say.

If a speaker has reason to be thankful for the opportunity of addressing a group, it is quite in order for him to say so in a formal and intelligent manner. Suppose he has been permitted to speak to some group on a project in which he is deeply interested. It might be the Red Cross or the Community Chest, or a project to establish a new park. It is a project in which he believes, and for which he wishes to gain support. Thus, when he comes to the end of the speech, he may very properly say, "I appreciate the privilege of presenting my ideas on this matter and thank you for your attention and for the opportunity to address you." This does not weaken the effect of his speech.

But if he soars to oratorical heights and exhorts the crowd, "Let's all get together and push this project to a glorious completion! Thank you"—he has not added substantially to the effect of his words.

(Sept. 1959, p.18)

THE SPEAKER TAKES A TEXT

The clergyman goes to his Bible for his sermon text, and for illustrations to illuminate his thought.

So the public speaker in any field may very well go to his collection of quotations for a text or for testimonial support, illustrations, or ideas on his theme.

Patient, painstaking writers, like Bartlett, Edwards and Douglas, have labored to collect these quotations for us, and to classify them, dictionary fashion, for easy reference. Every speaker should have such a collection at his hand.

Suppose, for instance, that I am to deliver a speech on some occasion which calls for the expression of patriotic fervor, or love of country, or devotion to its ideals. The theme has been discussed so often that there is little left to originality. I should have to follow some more or less well beaten path, but perhaps I can give it an unexpected turn.

What have the eloquent thinkers of the past said about it?

Turning to my book of quotations, under the heading of patriotism I find Cicero's wise words: "Our country is the common parent of all."

That makes us one big family, and so the words of Virgil are suitable for use: "The noblest motive is the public good." That is a fine one to toss to our politicians. And speaking of politicians, here is a good time to quote President Rutherford B. Hayes: "He serves his party best who serves his country best."

45

This line appears to lead to something worthwhile. I can stress service to my fellow men as a service to my nation, and I can call upon the leaders of my political party to join in that service. Rufus Choate said: "We join ourselves to no party that does not carry the flag and keep step to the music of the Union." Alongside that one we may place the words of Shakespeare: "Be just and fear not; let all the ends thou aimest at be thy country's, thy God's and truth's."

But I must not devote all my speech to politicians. The individual citizen has responsibilities, as suggested by Goethe: "In peace patriotism really consists only in this—that everyone sweeps before his own door, minds his own business, also learns his own lesson, that it may be well with him in his own house."

And now I am well on my way with a speech that shall stir my hearers. Here are three points which can be assembled into one sensible, rather useful talk, without losing all opportunity for a bit of eloquence, and with a measure of difference from the conventional flag waving.

If I need additional encouragement in its development, I can return to the book of quotations and search further under such headings as "Nation," "Native Land," "Freedom," "Peace" and other related themes. I can refer freely, but not excessively, to the wisdom of the ancients, with real benefit to my address.

Perhaps I am required to make a speech about speaking, or oratory. Will the book of quotations help me?

I start by looking under the heading of "Oratory."

Here I discover the words of Lord Cecil: "Eloquence is vehement simplicity." With it there is the line from Thomas Gray: "Thoughts that breathe and words that burn." Cicero contributes: "Brevity is a great praise of eloquence."

This reminds me that there are words of warning to be spoken to the aspirant orator, and so I pick up Montesquieu: "What the orators want in depth, they give you in length." And Prior pipes up with: "It is remarkable that they talk most who have the least to say." Then comes Chesterfield, saying: "The manner of your speaking is full as important as the matter."

Here we have another suggested speech outline, under three main headings. First, we are reminded that brevity is essential. Then we note that we must have something to say. Third, there is the thought that the manner of speaking, the "eloquent simplicity," is to be sought.

Almost any student of speech can get a good talk out of that.

These are just two samples of what your book of quotations can do for you when you find your springs of originality running dry. All we have to do is to pick up good ideas from quotable writers, and weave them into our own thinking. Presently we shall come up with a speech so good that it will impress our hearers, and possibly do them some good.

It is to be hoped that you will use this technique in your own speech preparation. Do not be afraid of being accused of plagiarism. You can profit by the wisdom of others, and you can give them full credit. Thus you will acquire an air of wide reading, and an acquaintance with the great ones of the past.

Most of the people whom you address have never heard of some of those whom you will quote. Perhaps you had not heard of them yourself until you began this study. Of course you recognize such names as Cicero and Goethe and Gladstone, but what about Pascal and Trench and Warwick and Joubert? Even though you cannot locate them with exactness as to time and place, you can accept their helpful thoughts, and so will others to whom you quote them.

Most of today's originality is in the use we make of what our forebears have said or written. Much of their thinking is unknown to those whom we address. We do our listeners a favor when we bring them the wisdom of the ancients through direct quotations.

Quote freely and with accuracy. Use the quotations where they will best fit. Use them, above all else, to stimulate your own thinking.
(March 1955, pp. 27-28)

SO YOU HAVE TO MAKE A SPEECH?
O.K.—TAKE A SUBJECT!

Talk about your own business. Find speech material in your daily work.

Any man who follows an honorable and productive occupation has at his hand a fund of lively, interesting and useful material for his speeches. Let him use a bit of imagination and originality along with observation, and speech themes will fairly leap at him.

The shelves of any grocery store teem with good suggestions for study. The hardware store is a veritable museum of human history and progress in invention. The tables and show cases in the dry goods store are loaded with stories.

The history of silk and of linen, two of the oldest fabrics, will repay study and will work into a speech of absorbing interest. Cotton and wool, the grading of cloth, the count of linen threads, the weaving of patterns, and a score of other trade matters will provide inspiration for many speeches.

The professional man is surrounded by speech materials, on his own desk or in his office.

The civil engineer can recount the story of some great construction enterprise, such as Boulder Dam, or the Eiffel Tower, or the Galveston Seawall, or the pyramids of Egypt. He can explain the construction of a modern highway or a railroad, or he can describe the building of a bridge. Why does a building not fall down? What are the values of reinforced concrete? Discuss the spider as a construction expert. These are a few of the items which would be of interest to every intelligent person, if they are well presented.

The chemist and the physicist have a tremendous volume of material. Consider modern progress in science, in the revealing of nature's secrets. Take a textbook in chemistry or physics written in 1900, and compare it with one of the present day. Observe the number of new elements which have been discovered, and the new reactions which have been brought into use.

The whole field of atomic research and of nuclear reactions is open to the student. It provides an inexhaustible supply of material for the imagination.

The chemist might take for his speech title, "Magic in the Test Tube" and build up a most attractive offering, without going beyond his own laboratory.

The lawyer and the doctor have in their possession facts which are not only full of interest, but which are of definite value to every listener. The attorney can do good service and attract favorable attention by talking about "How to Make Your Will" or "Don't Die Intestate." He can tell his audience how to keep out of jail, or how to safeguard the title to property, or any one of a dozen professional secrets good for the public to know.

The doctor has the vital facts about human health. He can discuss modern methods of medical practice as compared with those of ancient days. The medicine man of early times makes a good background for his successor, today's physician. People are interested in health and how to keep it. The doctor has the answers. Let him talk about them.

The banker and the economist have vast stores of interesting material, most of it unrecognized. Human nature as observed at the teller's window is interesting, informative and amusing. Every experienced banker has his fund of stories about peculiar customers.

The agriculturist, whether he be a farmer or a rancher, deals with supplies of food so vital to human life. The cornbelt farmer has a great story to talk about in the development of the modern hybrid strains of corn which have almost doubled production; industrial uses of the soy bean have revolutionized farming in some parts, but people generally do not know about it. Farm machinery of today, compared with that of fifty years ago, gives a story full of interest.

And so it goes, through all the occupations of men. The commonplace matters of daily life are strange and intriguing to those who do not know them. Every man has plenty of material in his own day's work, if he will use his imagination and his information, with a touch of originality in presenting the facts.

All this is of far more value than most of us realize, not only because of its interest, but also because our presentation of it creates understanding and good will on the part of the public. Talking about our own work builds good public relations.

Do not hesitate to talk shop. Do not make it your only theme, nor let it become boring. Let people know that you know other things than your daily work, but let them know at the same time that you do know your own business well enough to talk about it intelligently.

The things you know best may be the very best things for you to talk about.

(July 1955, pp. 6-7)

The Orderly Planning
of a Speech

The second area in speechmaking which comes to us within the classical pattern as Disposition or Arrangement is never neglected by modern scholars in their discussions of speech development. Dr. Smedley considered the organization of the speech to be of great importance. To quite an extent he was in agreement with most writers on rhetorical principles that the purpose toward which the speech was directed should influence the basic organizational pattern.

PURPOSE POINTS THE WAY

Purpose is the controlling factor in life.

Purpose determines the goal, marks the path, and furnishes the motive power.

Purpose—some purpose—underlies character, culture, position, progress, every kind of achievement.

Purpose makes the speech.

There are four general classifications of purpose which govern the speaker. Once the general purpose of a speech has been settled upon, the type of presentation to be made should immediately be clear.

The four categories may be stated thus:

1. To inform or instruct.
2. To stimulate or inspire.
3. To persuade or convince.
4. To entertain or amuse.

The teacher, trying to unfold the mysteries of science or mathematics or history to a group of students, is seeking to bring about a reaction quite different from that sought by a legislator who advocates the adoption of some measure, or the political speaker who tries to win votes for his candidate.

The preacher, seeking to lead his hearers to a better life and to win them to the Christian way of thinking, has a purpose very much unlike that of the after-dinner speaker who is trying to amuse an audience, or the entertainer who is expected to be funny.

It is easy to see that the general purpose of the speech makes a vast difference in the construction and presentation of the material. When the speaker starts to prepare his speech, one of his first problems

—perhaps the very first one—is to analyze the occasion, the audience, and the purpose so as to decide whether he must seek to inform or inspire, to persuade, entertain, or stir to action. Not until this point is settled can he build his speech to produce the desired effect.

The second step as to purpose is to determine the specific purpose to be achieved.

The political speaker knows exactly what he wants to accomplish. He is after votes, and his whole effort will be concentrated on that end.

The salesman wants to get the order—make the sale—get the name on the dotted line. His specific purpose is clear.

Whatever the definite purpose, the speaker must know it, and he must build his speech so as to make the audience understand what he is after.

No speaker has a right to waste the time of an audience if he does not know just what he is trying to accomplish. If his aim is not clear to him, you may depend upon it that he will leave his hearers equally in the dark.

A clergyman who belongs to a Toastmasters Club had his mind directed to the importance of making the purpose clear one Sunday morning when he talked with one of his members, also a Toastmaster, at the close of the service.

"How was the sermon, speaking as a Toastmasters evaluator?" he inquired.

"It was a fine speech," his fellow Toastmaster replied. "It was well constructed, and well delivered. Your language was excellent. There were no distressing grunts nor hesitations. Your gestures were just about right. But, Parson, what did you want us to do about it? You never told us that."

Undoubtedly the purpose was somewhere in the preacher's mind, but he did not get it over to his audience. The people approved of what he said, and enjoyed listening to him, but he did not land the order because he did not tell them what to do. Multitudes of speakers, preachers and otherwise, have the same fault in their speeches.

When you prepare a speech, purpose is the first thing to consider. It will guide you in choosing material and arranging it. It will dictate the opening and the closing of your speech. It will be your control throughout the preparation and the delivery.

Get the purpose fixed in your own mind with great clarity. Then make it equally clear to your audience, and let them know just what you want them to do. If they then fail to act as you have urged, at least it will not be your fault.

"The secret of success is constancy to purpose," said Disraeli,

and his words apply to your speech as well as to your entire career.
(Oct. 1950, pp. 1-2)

BUILDING A SPEECH

The process of constructing a useful outline for a speech is one of the more tiresome tasks of the speaker. This is one reason why many speeches are poorly constructed. It is just too much trouble.

As a help to the man who wishes to learn how to organize his thoughts logically, here is a sketch of the preparatory work for a speech on the theme, "Success."

What shall be our purpose? Shall we tell how to succeed, or what constitutes success, or shall we tell about people who have been successful?

Considering the general interest in "how to" prescriptions, we may choose for our subject: "How to be Successful."

First, we may begin by reminding our hearers that one of the dominant desires of mankind is to be successful.

Second, what is success?

(a) It may be the attainment of a position above mediocrity, at least in one's particular activity;

(b) It may be the satisfaction of one's ambitions and aspirations.

Here we need some illustrations. Some people are ambitious to win success in some inferior line of activity. Consider the small boy whose ambition was to be able to wiggle his ears. He spent much time on this, and when he managed to produce a slight movement of his external auditory apparatus, he claimed success.

Third, success is always relative. It depends on circumstances. It may involve the acquisition of wealth, gaining social prominence, occupational proficiency, home relationships. The nature of success depends on the purpose of the striver for attainment.

Fourth, we consider the "secrets" of success. How is it to be gained? Several factors are involved: health, character, appearance, personality, knowledge of job, efficiency in work, interest in work, ability to use brains, ability to get along with people.

We shall select two or three of these for special emphasis.

Fifth, consider whether there is a single determinant in the struggle for success. Can we select one *sine qua non,* one essential, without which success is impossible?

We may say the most important determinant is the emotional make-up, the personality traits.

Experts have surveyed the field, and they say that knowledge and skill constitute about one-half of the equipment for success, while the other fifty percent takes in behavior, disposition, mental attitudes, cooperativeness, ability to get along with others.

Says one authority: "It is better for business and social advancement to have a good personality and mediocre ability than to possess a superior intellect and ability, along with a displeasing personality."

Sixth, with all this material, we have laid the foundation for a powerful conclusion—an appeal for the cultivation of those personality traits which are so essential. This conclusion should be so clear and strong that action will be the natural result.

And now, what is the matter with this outline?

It is too long. It takes too much material. It is timed for twenty to thirty minutes, which might be all right for a commencement address, but is far beyond the limits for a short speech. We must shorten it, by elimination and condensation.

This is one of the hardest tasks for the speaker. He has so much good material, and he hesitates to leave out any of it. One is reminded of the saying of the gardener: "When you plant lettuce, sow thick and thin quick." Apply that principle to this outline, and you will get results.

But remember that it is better to have more material than you can cover than it is to run out of thoughts when you are only half through your time.

One of the best examples of a short speech, based on a scarcity of material, is found in the story of a young man attending a theological school in preparation for entering the ministry. In the class in pulpit oratory in which he was enrolled, the assignment one day was for each student to accept a text or subject as he mounted the platform, and then delivered a sermon on it without time for preparation.

Our young friend, as he stepped forward, was handed a slip of paper with the one word, "Zaccheus," written on it.

Being short of stature, he had to stand on tiptoe to look over the lectern. As he stood there, he declaimed, "My sermon is divided into three parts. First, Zaccheus was a little man. So am I. Second, Zaccheus was up a tree. So am I. Third, Zaccheus made haste to come down. And so will I."

The essential point is to have a clear outline, or framework, on which you can hang as much material as you wish, depending on the length of time allotted to your talk. You can then build it up with illustrations and analogies and arguments, or you can trim it down with all necessary severity. The clear outline leads to a definite conclusion, and the length of time it takes for you to reach the conclusion depends on the amount of detail with which you fill in. Just be sure that your plan is clearly in your mind, and that your purpose dominates the conclusion of your speech.

(Nov. 1957, pp. 14-15)

ALL TALKING IS PUBLIC SPEAKING, SO...IT PAYS TO PLAN

Most of our talking is public speaking.

Whether we address one person or one hundred, our words become public when we utter them.

In our speaking, we may be brilliant, entertaining, enlightening or dull, prosy, uninteresting and boring, no matter how many hearers we have.

Whether we are speaking to individuals or to groups, the same fundamental rules apply. This is fortunate for the public speaker, for it enables him to practice public speaking in every conversation.

Good speech is planned, whether it be for the large audience or the small one. A good talker does not sound off indiscriminately. In discussion he has to think quickly, but even so he does not talk without thinking. If he does, he may have cause later to regret his haste.

In most of our talking, it is possible to plan quickly what we are about to say, and to give some thought as to how we shall say it. Such planning helps us to avoid the poor enunciation, construction and choice of words which may otherwise mar our conversation. We would hardly be likely to say, "I'm just gunnergo crost uh street" if we had given a moment's thought to it.

We would avoid embarrassing remarks, such as mentioning a projected trip to Reno when talking to a recently divorced friend, if we had given a moment's consideration to what it implied.

Planning, or thinking ahead, helps us to eliminate the grunts and extra syllables which so many of us use, especially in getting started. Note how many times you start a sentence with "Well-uh," or "Uh-now" and similar exordial words.

Watch telephone talking, either your own or that of other people. Do you know of anyone who habitually begins with "Ah-h-is this ah-the Smith-Jones-uh office-uh?" Perhaps he carries on with "Well-uh, I wanted to talk-uh to ah-h Mr. Smith-uh. Is he-uh around the office-uh?"

It might have been better if he had used the time wasted in hesitation, in thinking ahead so that when the clerk said, "This is the Smith-Jones Company," he would have replied immediately, "May

I speak to Mr. Smith, please?"

Again, good speech involves having something to say. If we applied that rule to our daily talking, it would eliminate at least thirty percent of it. When applied to public speech, it might exclude from ten to twenty percent, for many speakers introduce so much extraneous matter into their speeches that they run short of time in which to say something that really matters.

Once again, if we have something worth saying, that something deserves to be well spoken. When we say "well spoken," we include choice and arrangement of words, pronunciation, enunciation, voice quality and other elements of good speech. All these matters can be practiced in conversation.

There is one more element in talking which is too frequently overlooked. That is the matter of listening.

An excellent rule is to devote at least as much time to listening as to speaking. This is especially desirable in conversation. It is only fair to give the others a chance to say something.

Many of us resemble the lady who was calling on a friend. Her little daughter accompanied her. The child wished to say something, but the ladies were busy talking. Finally the child broke in on the conversation. Her mother rebuked her. "You must never interrupt when others are talking," she said. "You must wait till we get through."

"But mother," the child wailed, "you never get through!"

One of the difficulties in improving our conversational habits is that we must, as a rule, be our own critic. It is a delicate matter for another person to give us an honest criticism of our talking. We can secure competent evaluation for our public speaking, but even our best friend hesitates to tell us just how boring and useless our "small talk" becomes.

Our way to improvement in conversation is through honest self-evaluation. We need to watch ourselves, as objectively as possible, and find out how we can do better.

Constant watchfulness will enable any talker to improve his talking, whether to individuals or from the platform, for a good conversational style is reflected in better platform speaking.

(Nov. 1956, pp. 7-8)

TALKING IS SELLING

All talking is selling and all selling involves talking, whether it is written or oral.

In all our talking, we are attempting to "sell" information or ideas or inspiration, or some other intangible. Of course, I am using the word "sell" in a very broad sense, not limiting it to financial or commodity transactions. A common purpose underlies all these matters of communications, whether we are presenting ideas for acceptance, or groceries or other goods for purchase.

When you are trying to sell an automobile, a house, an insurance policy, or a television set, you have in mind from the beginning the purpose which you hope to accomplish. That purpose is to get the listener's name on the order blank, or his check for the down payment. Your talk is directed to the accomplishment of that purpose. If your selling talk is successful, you will get the order. Your customer's reaction will serve as the evaluation for your effort.

Similarly, when you address an audience, whether of one or two, or of a hundred people, you are trying to accomplish something, and your speech must be directed to that end. When you speak at your Toastmasters Club meeting, one purpose is to gain experience, but if your experience is to be worthwhile, you must be trying to accomplish still further results in informing or inspiring your audience, or inspiring them to action, or perhaps entertaining them. If you have a definite, well-defined purpose in mind, you will naturally be in earnest as you talk, and being in earnest is essential to good speaking.

Our familiar "A-I-D-A" formula for speech organization is based on the salesmanship procedure, and it works as well in selling ideas as in selling goods.

The speaker or the salesman must gain favorable Attention. Then he must arouse Interest. Third, he creates Desire; and finally, he leads to Action. There you have it: "A-I-D-A."

If you are making a speech intended to win votes or other favorable action, you can use this formula with good effect, provided you bring to it the elements of conviction, knowledge and sincerity. These elements will result in enthusiasm, which is so essential in all kinds of selling.

You must know your subject. You must be convinced of the worth of what you are advocating. You must sincerely believe in what you say, if you are to lead your hearers to believe in it. When you do have these qualities of knowledge, conviction and belief, your delivery will give evidence of your sincerity through the enthusiasm you will display.

The "sales talk," in the wider meaning of the term, is the one which you will most frequently have occasion to use, and you will do well to study the technique.

In general, you will first sell yourself on the proposition, and then you will take the considerations which cause you to believe in it, and arrange them in a logical, convincing style, which will lead your audience to accept them and to act as you want them to.

In this as in every speech, always finish with a clear statement as to just what you want them to do about it. Never overlook the "so what." It belongs in every speech.

(Sept. 1960, pp. 28-29)

"Style has no fixed laws; it is changed by the usage of the people, never the same for any length of time."

—SENECA

Speech Style and Language

The third area of speechmaking that has always been of concern to major writers on public address is that of the language, style, and the semantic aspects of expression. Dr. Smedley considered these to be of principal importance. He sought not only to be correct and effective in his own style of writing and speaking but also to encourage all Toastmasters to improve their own. Nearly a third of his writings on speechmaking that appeared in The Toastmaster *magazine related to this area. The following articles merely sample the idea that he considered to be of most importance.*

RIGHT SPEAKING...

If you would have a simple rule
A cultured man to tell,
Take notice: Does he always speak
His native language well?

The Toastmasters Club is dedicated to the cause of better speech. Every member is supposed to be on the alert to improve his forms of expression. He, of all persons, should "always speak his language well."

But what is the standard by which you are to judge his speech? How will you determine whether he is speaking well or ill? Is it that he agrees with you in his pronunciation or choice of words? But are you sure that you are right?

The trouble is that people do not speak alike, even though they use the same language, and they do not agree as to which is right or wrong.

Millions of people use the so-called English language. They can read it with a fair degree of understanding, except where different meanings are given to the same word in different localities, but when they speak it, their differences are notable. English as spoken in Great Britain or in Australia shows many variations from the same language in the United States. Even in the U.S.A. the accents and pronunciations are unlike in different regions.

CAN YOU TALK ENGLISH?

The fact that English may be your native language does not guarantee that you can speak it well.

But whether you speak it well or badly, your speech gives you away to every discerning listener. Every time you talk, every time you write, you reveal what you are. Your use of speech either helps or hinders you by its unfailing revelation.

When you use the wrong word, when you mispronounce a word, when you violate the common rules of grammar, when you use trite, commonplace words, you handicap yourself. You give yourself a low rating which may or may not be deserved.

Thousands of people make mistakes in their ordinary speech, and don't know it. Their friends are too polite to tell them. And they are too careless to watch themselves. They use common words, flat, colorless, and use even these without thought of rules of grammar. Some of them try to liven up their talk by use of profanity, vulgarity, or cheap, popular slang, thus still further reducing scanty vocabularies, and making their speech even less inspiring.

When it comes to writing, the picture is just as bad. Misspelled words add their influence to the misuse of grammatical forms and the use of wrong words. A letter which is poorly worded, incorrectly spelled, or illegibly written, defeats its purpose on the start. On the other hand, a letter which shows expert handling of language has a balance in its favor from the start.

Speech is largely a matter of habit, and to form correct habits of speech is little harder, if it is harder at all, than to fall into careless ways. This is one reason why slovenly speech is so great a handicap to the one who wishes to get ahead in life. It reveals habits of carelessness and laziness which extend to other matters than speech, and it may be a warning signal to the observant person on whom the speaker's advancement depends.

When you talk, you give yourself away. You reveal your true character in a picture which is more true and realistic than anything an artist can do for you. Better check up on your English. Maybe you will not be flattered by the self-painted picture you are showing to your associates.

If your mistakes are caused by ignorance, you owe it to yourself to gain information, such as is no further away than your City Library or High School. If carelessness is the cause of your slips in speech, then—well, maybe you can afford it. Most of us can't.

(May 1945, p. 17)

WHAT DO YOU REALLY MEAN?

Every word has at least three meanings.

First, there is the meaning in the mind of the one who speaks.

Second, there is the meaning which the word arouses in the mind of the hearer.

Third, there is the meaning inherent in the word, by reason of its derivation or usage.

If all three meanings agree, as they usually do not, it is fortunate. It makes for understanding. It is their mutual disagreement which causes confusion and misunderstanding.

When a speaker uses a certain word, he uses it because it names a certain idea or concept which he has in his own mind. When the word strikes the ear of another person, it brings up some idea or picture which may or may not be the same as that in the speaker's mind.

If the hearer's concept differs from that of the speaker, misunderstanding inevitably results.

Only when both speaker and hearer have the same understanding of the word is accurate communication possible to them. It happens all too often that both parties interpret the word in some way foreign to its true meaning. Then confusion is worse.

A word is merely the name or symbol of a mental concept. It does not necessarily describe the idea or object for which it stands. As is so clearly pointed out by Dr. Hans Oertel, a word does not really become a symbol until it ceases to describe. Dr. Oertel holds that a name or word is not descriptive of the object any more than a wardrobe check is descriptive of the coat or hat for which it calls.

This is why it becomes so important for every user of words to be sure that both he and his hearer have the same ideas in connection with the words they use.

Our word concepts vary according to our disposition, our environment, our experience, our education.

Consider some very common words. What picture is brought to your mind by such words as capitalism, communism, lobby, bureau, strike?

If you are a baseball player or a bowler, your idea of a "strike" is very different from that of a trades unionist. If you are a hotel keeper, your thought of "lobby" or of "bureau" is not at all like that of a politician.

What does red bring to your mind? To you it may suggest bright color, but to another it may mean anarchy, or extreme radicalism, or terrorism. More recently, it may symbolize the flag of one of the United Nations.

Mark Twain used to complain that there was only one word in the German language which was at all familiar to him. That word was damit, and he said that even that one was spelled wrong. When he used the word which those letters spelled for him, he meant something far different from what was meant by his German friend who spoke it.

Word meanings are never static. Changing conditions require changing meanings, even for the same word. The dictionary tries to record the best and most acceptable meanings. If we follow the dictionary, we can be reasonably safe. That is why it is important to refer frequently to authority for word meanings. That is why a dictionary has to be revised at frequent intervals.

If we make sure that both we and our hearers use the same authority on meanings, we can make ourselves understood. Otherwise we may be in the situation of Humpty Dumpty, who said, "My words mean whatever I mean them to mean."

(Nov. 1945, pp. 15-16)

OUR CHANGING LANGUAGE

Our language is constantly in a state of change. Words fluctuate in meaning. Usages which were unacceptable become standard practice. New words are introduced, and old ones become obsolete.

The dictionary makers have to put out a new revised edition every two or three years to keep up with the changes, and the careful word user must carry on a ceaseless study of the new dictionaries if he will hold his place as a user of correct speech. But this fact need not cause us distress.

Change is an element of life, and so long as a language is living and in use change is inevitable. People just can't leave the language alone.

Latin, for us, is a "dead language"—not dead and buried, but dead in the sense that it is completed, finished, no longer subject to change. That is why it can be made the language of science and philosophy. It stays fixed in its form and implications, and so it can be made to express exact and stable meanings.

In the days when Latin was the daily speech of a great people, it was just as filled with changes and shifts in forms and meanings as our own language is today. Thus, we find Quintilian, writing nearly two thousand years ago, crying out against errors in the Latin which are strangely suggestive of the strictures of present-day advocates of correct speech.

The every-day man in the street was quite as slangy and careless in his use of the classic language as we are now in our common talk. Only when it ceased to be a popularly spoken tongue did its forms become crystallized and set in permanent molds. Because it is a "dead language" it is no longer subject to growth and change.

Much as we may disapprove of the careless speech of the common American, we must not forget to be glad that our language is still capable of change. Its growth is a constant reminder of its life and virility. The addition of new words and the changing meanings given to old words are evidence of our own intellectual progress.

This principle of change adds to the difficulty of the careful speaker. It is very difficult to hit on word uses which can be cited as inflexible, not subject to change, absolutely right. Every rule may have its exception, and about the time you think you have a word nailed down where it cannot possibly wriggle loose, you find that someone has released it to some new, different, and even technically illegal use. We can't keep the language from changing. Our best course is to adapt our own speech to fit the changes.

(Jan. 1945, p.9)

CHRISTMAS WORDS...

A festival such as Christmas, observed by multitudes of people all over the world, and for nearly twenty centuries, must have a wealth of picturesque words in the background.

The name of the festival itself is suggestive. It is composed of two words, "Christ" and "mas." The old Anglo Saxon form was "Cristes Maesse," which simply means "Christ's festival," just as we have candlemass and Michaelmas and many other ecclesiastical celebrations.

There is interest in the name "Christ," which is really the official or ceremonial title applied to the Savior. "Jesus" was his family name, by which His family and friends knew Him. The Greek Christos is a translation of the Hebrew Messias, which means to anoint or consecrate. Thus the title "Christ" designates the mission of Jesus.

In the early days of the Christian era, when to admit that one was a follower of the Faith was to invite persecution, the early church resorted to various symbols to represent their fellowship and the name of their Leader. The initial letters of the Greek word were commonly used for that purpose. These letters, chi and rho, in their Greek form look like our X and U, and I suppose that it was the ancient use of the X from which gave rise to the unpleasant custom which prevails today of using "Xmas" as a substitute for "Christmas."

63

The date of the Christmas observance was long a problem. It is impossible to determine what was the exact day on which Jesus was born, and there has been great diversity of opinion about it. Dates have been set in January, March, April and May at various times, but in the middle of the Fourth Century, Pope Julius officially decreed that December 25 should be observed as the birthday, and it has been so ever since.

In the early days, the observance was counted a heathen custom, and the church did not favor it. As the custom grew in popularity, certain practices were carried over from ancient heathen religions, until Christmas observance became a strange mixture of Christian and pagan customs, all combined to honor the coming of the Prince of Peace. There may be something symbolic in the fact that these customs are so widely representative, so diverse in their origin, since Jesus counted Himself the Saviour of all mankind.

Christmas has been regarded with suspicion and disfavor by some Christian groups. For instance, Christmas was officially abolished in 1643 by Cromwell's Roundhead Parliament, the laws making it a felony to observe the day in any manner, even by abstaining from work. The General Court of Massachusetts, in 1659, under the Puritan influence, decreed that any person celebrating the Christmas occasion should be heavily fined. Fortunately, those old ideas have passed away, or we should miss a great deal of the joy of living and giving.

The mistletoe custom, with its privilege to lovers, is a carry-over of an ancient Druid custom. Among those primitive inhabitants of Briton the mistletoe was sacred as a symbol of privilege or indulgence. It was gathered with impressive ceremonies and carried in the temple processionals which celebrated the changing of the seasons. In its presence many of the restrictions of ordinary life were laid aside and people indulged themselves without restraint. The mistletoe was especially friendly to lovers, and our references to kissing under the mistletoe of today are a reminiscence of that Druidical saturnalia.

The "yule log" is another Anglo-Saxon relic. What it means is in doubt. "Yule" may come from the old Anglo-Saxon word for "Wheel," and its use may have been tied in with the turning or wheeling of the seasons. The winter solstice was observed by the Druids, who announced the advent of the season by rolling down hill a flaming wheel of wood. It was considered good luck to secure a brand from this burning wheel with which to light the hearthfire at home. This may be the origin of our custom of bringing in a great log at Christmas, to burn in the fireplace for days.

Of course, there are other possible derivations of "yule," and it is impossible to determine whether it is from an old Norse word jol, which was the name of a pagan festival, or from the Icelandic Ylir, the name of a winter month, or from the Old French joli, which is the root of our familiar "jolly."

The French word for Christmas is Noel, a word made familiar to us through the old carol, "The first Noel the angels did say." The word is apparently derived from the Latin natus, meaning born.

These are only a few of the many Christmas words. All of them have an interesting history and background.

(Dec. 1947, pp.1-2)

WORDS—WHAT ARE THEY?

Words are poetry.

Words are music.

Words are pictures.

Words are concentrated crystallized history.

But, fundamentally, words are grunts.

An intelligible word consists of a combination of vowel and consonant sounds. The vowel is distinguished from the consonant because the vowel, or vocal, sound can be produced independently, while the consonant (sounding with) can be properly produced only in connection with a vowel sound. It is the addition of the consonant— the direction or modification by tongue, teeth, lips and breath—which makes possible the vast vocabularies of today's speech.

The development of language may be traced in some measure in the experience of the human infant. As the baby tries to make sympathetic adults understand his wants and wishes, his first vocal efforts are in the form of inarticulate yells, grunts, squeals or cooing sounds. It does not require a great deal of experience for him to learn to associate certain results with certain sounds. Probably that is why he cries when he is cross or hungry or in pain. He knows that crying will bring attention; therefore, he cries.

After a time, he learns to make certain lip sounds, never realizing that he is rehearsing the experience of mankind in discovering articulation. In due course, he learns to talk, adding words to his vocabulary as he needs them, just as his forebears have done from the earliest antiquity.

Civilization and speech have grown up together. They are mutually dependent. Civilization is impossible without some form of communication, and the exchange of ideas, by means of speech, makes possible the advancement of mankind in what we call civilized interests and occupations.

(March 1950, pp. 1-2)

BETTER VOCABULARIES—WHY?

There is a great deal of interest in vocabulary building and improvement.

Likewise, there appears to be a general misunderstanding about it, both as to purpose and method.

In recent years there have been published and sold great numbers of books on how to build better vocabularies, and yet there is no great improvement to be noted by the careful observer. Something is wrong.

Apparently, many people have the idea that possession of a book on words automatically results in better speech. Finding that it takes work and study, they lose their enthusiasm. Many others are unable to understand just why they need vocabulary enlargement. These are not good students.

It should be understood that studies in vocabulary building definitely are not for the purpose of loading one with a lot of big words, seldom needed. The study need not deal with big words at all, except as one's thoughts require polysyllabic expression.

There are two fundamental reasons for building better vocabularies.

First, the process helps us to read or listen with better understanding.

Second, it enables us to express our own thoughts more clearly.

These two reasons are your incentive for working on your vocabulary.

With more than half a million words in the language, you will do very well if you understand so much as five percent of them. Anyone who knows ten percent is in the superman class.

But if you do not have a fair understanding of at least 15,000 words, you are under a handicap when you read or listen, for much of what is said will go right past you.

You can get along fairly well in ordinary speech with a stock of two or three thousand words. If that is the case, and if your thinking is not deeply involved, you may be satisfied with these. But if you are to be an intelligent reader of newspapers, magazines and books, you must know many more words with reasonable accuracy.

Unless you are a scientist, or in one of the learned professions, it is quite unlikely that you will need to speak such words as biotics, amylaceous, endocrinology, stereophonic, microclimatology, chiaroscuro, and many others which sound wonderful and mean nothing to most people.

You may never need even to mention herpetology, plenary, ecumenical, speleology, or numismatics, but you may run across these last-mentioned words, and if you do not know in some measure what they mean, they will mean nothing at all to you.

Be as simple as you like in your speech, so long as you make yourself understood; but be very sure that you have enough words to express yourself adequately.

It is not the size of the words that counts, but the clearness with which they represent your thoughts. Probably you can get along with a speaking vocabulary in which there is not a word of more than three syllables. If you can do that without cheating yourself, by all means do it.

But you cannot get along as an intelligent listener or reader unless you know the meaning of a very large number of words of all sizes and sounds.

Most people use a very limited range of words, and overwork these. Set yourself to the task of building up your stock of words. Start with these simple methods:

1. Stop overworking certain favorite words. Everyone has a list of pet words which he uses to excess. Thus he not only weakens his speech, but tires those who hear him. Any word becomes a bad word when used too often.

2. Get acquainted with new words. You encounter them daily, over the air, in newspapers and magazines, in conversation. When you hear a new word which sounds promising, make it your own. Use it.

3. See how many words you can find to express the same thought. For example, list all the words which suggest to you the thought of a house, such as residence, shelter, shack, etc. Don't stop until you have listed 12 or 15 words.

4. Refer to the sports pages of a newspaper. Observe how many different ways the writer finds to say that the batter hit the ball, or that the runner made his base. Note the use of lively words, picture words, exciting words. Learn to choose vigorous, vital words, which carry their own punch.

5. As you add new words, be careful how you use them. There are three things you must know about a word before you can safely make use of it: (a) How is it pronounced? (b) What does it mean? (c) Where should it be used?

(June 1964, p. 10)

Stop Me If—

Dr. Smedley's writings on humor and the importance of humor to the public speaker can best be described within his concept of language and style.

> *"Whatever trouble Adam had,*
> *No man, in days of yore*
> *Could say, when he had told a joke,*
> *I've heard that one before."*

There are no new jokes. We have a dozen or so comical situations, recognized by all ethical jokers, and all our wit and humor revolve around them. Since man first learned to laugh, he has laughed at these things. Each generation takes up the old ideas, dresses them in modern styles, adapts them to modern conditions, rewords them, and then passes them out for new. But they are the same old jokes, after all.

The salvation of the after-dinner speaker lies in the fact that the oldest joke may be new to someone. In every audience there are those who have heard the story before—perhaps many times before—but there are also those to whom it is new. Thus, those who know the joke laugh at their old friend, or out of politeness, or just from sheer boredom, to cover up their yawns, while the others welcome it as a novel jest.

> *"A jest's prosperity lies in the ear of him who hears it:*
> *Never in the tongue*
> *Of him who makes it."*

With this Shakespearian authority, let no one hesitate to use a pointed story, however old and familiar it be to some. Depend upon it, someone in the audience will hear it for the first time, and by his pleasure he will give the old joke a new lease on life.

That our jokes are old ones is demonstrated in the collections of facetiae which have been made through the ages. The one best known in English is "Joe Miller's Jest Book," which was published in 1739. In its original form it was a mere compilation of witticisms drawn by the versatile John Mottley mostly from 16th and 17th century jest books, the very best joke in it being the name of Joe Miller. He was a professional comedian of the 17th century who, in spite of his profession, is said never to have made up a joke in his life. He merely told them. Because of the use Mottley made of his name, "Joe Miller" stands to this day as a synonym for stale jokes, while few of us have ever heard the name of the man who wrote the book.

There just aren't any new jokes. Our fun comes to us from remotest antiquity, from the Indian, the Syriac, the Hebrew, the

Arabic, the Persian, the Greek and the Roman, and where they got the ideas we can only guess. But jokes which have survived the ages and have been found amusing by our ancestors since the dawning of human intelligence must be good. They ought to be good enough for us, at least until we can invent some new ones, so let us use them freely and without fear.

There is always someone to whom your story is new, so tell it to him. Tell the story well, with few words, in an appropriate place. Never drag a joke in by main strength just for the sake of telling it. If it does not illuminate the point at issue, leave it out. And don't begin with "Stop me if you've heard this one" or you will get to tell very few of your jokes.

(April 1941, pp. 1-4)

MUST YOU TELL A STORY?...

If you aspire to be a popular speaker, you will have to learn to tell stories.

Then, if you create a reputation as a story-telling speaker, you will have to live up to it, which lays a heavy responsibility on you.

Even the most serious speaker needs to be able to light up his discourse with occasional flashes of wit and humor, which may or may not be provided by the use of stories, and so the answer to the title question must be in the affirmative. You must tell a story now and then.

This brings up several important questions.

When should you tell a story?

How should you tell a story?

Where can you find good stories?

How can you remember the stories after finding them?

WHEN?

There are at least three occasions when a story is appropriate.

First, to put over an argument without using a whole chapter of serious talk. Consider how effectively Abraham Lincoln used homely stories, usually with the result that an argument was refuted or a point illuminated with very few words.

But the story must be pertinent. It must bear directly on what you are saying. An "illustration" must illuminate. An inappropriate story may raise a laugh, but it weakens your speech.

Second, to keep your speech from growing too serious, too intense. The grave-digging scene which opens the fourth act of Hamlet is a good example. Shakespeare deliberately introduces the clowns to relieve the tension of tragedy. It is excellent speech technique—if well handled.

Third, to catch the attention of the audience at the start of your speech, and to establish a desirable rapport, a harmony between speaker and audience, which can lead naturally into attentive listening. This is not always the best practice, and if used at all, it must be with discretion and good judgment. But the experienced speaker learns to judge his audience and the level of its attention, so that he knows when to use this trick, and how to use it, as well as when to skip it.

But the very best place to find stories and illustrations is in your own experience.

Things which happened to you and which can be told in the first person are good material. They have the added advantage that they are your own, so no one else can use them unless and until he gets them from you.

There is always value in telling a story in the first person, if you can do so without getting into embarrassment. If you can use it as something a friend said to you on the way downtown, or as a bright remark of your wife or as some childhood experience of your own, it is especially good.

Better leave radio jokes alone, for almost everyone else has heard them too. Don't discard a good story simply because it is old. There is always someone to whom it may be new.

You can test every story in your repertoire by these simple standards:

1. Is it likely to prove objectionable to anyone? That is, does it offend anyone's race, religion or color?

2. Is it clean and decent? Shun anything that has even the slightest suggestion of being off-color.

3. Does the story amuse you after the fourth or fifth time? Or does it lose its effect after several readings or tellings? If you don't enjoy it, your audience will not care for it either.

4. Does it have a point which is clear and unmistakable—and worthwhile?

5. Can you tell it well?

REMEMBER?

You run across a good item in your reading, and you say to yourself, "That is a good one to use in my next speech." But you fail to clip it or make a note of it, and when you want it, it is gone from your memory. The moral is, don't depend on your memory alone.

Keep a notebook or a file of cards for this purpose. When you need an illustration, go to your collection and find it.

HOW?

Tell the story well. That is the universal and imperative rule.

You must know the story perfectly. You must have its procedure and its point thoroughly in mind, and you must have learned, by experience, what is the best way to put it over.

To learn this, you will need to have repeated it many times in conversation, watching to see how it works most effectively with the one or two people who hear it each time. Good story-telling takes practice.

A story is well told when it is condensed into brief form without losing the effectiveness of its point. Too many details will kill the best story.

The more naturally it can be woven into your speech, the better. Too much preliminary explanation or introduction will ruin the effect. If you can make it appear to be an essential part of your speech, it will be much stronger than if you have to bring it in with "That reminds me of a story I once heard," or some such cliche.

WHERE?

There are scores of joke books, anecdote books, collections of wit and humor.

Which one is best? I decline to answer. There is no "best" book of the sort.

When someone asks me what book of illustrations and stories he should buy, I reply by advising him to go to a public library and inspect for himself the shelf of books on wit and humor and jokes and after-dinner stories and speeches.

The seeker of humor should go through as many of these as he has time and patience for, then select the one which most appeals to him. It should be carefully indexed, both topically and as to source.

He should consult the topical index to see if his special lines of interest are covered. The bigness of the book is no criterion. Quality of material is the important thing.

Many good story-tellers use catchwords to suggest stories. Thus if something is said about education, or about criticism, or about errors in grammar, or about political candidates, or Irishmen, or automobiles, or apples, the word brings an appropriate story to mind. Hang your stories on to such catchwords and you will remember them.

SUMMARY

Decide when and why you need to tell a story; what effect you want to produce; what story fits the occasion; and then prepare carefully to tell it in the best possible style. Don't tell too many jokes, and when you do tell one, make it count.

(April 1947, pp. 17-19)

"All attempts at exciting the feelings must prove ineffectual, unless they be enlivened by the voice of the speaker, by his look, and by the action of almost his whole body."

—QUINTILIAN

Speech Presentation

Delivery is used to cover both the physical and the vocal aspects of speechmaking. This art has varied in the manner that it is described, but at no time in the course of the development of philosophies of public speaking has it been considered to be of minor importance. Dr. Smedley's writings show a considerable interest on his part in the way that ideas are presented to an audience. In general he incorporated the classical concept of memory and mastery of the material to be presented in this and the other aspects of speechmaking. In this respect he was "modern" in his attitude toward the "traditional."

THEY HEARD HIM GLADLY

The name of Jesus of Nazareth is not commonly found in the lists of great orators as set forth by historians of oratory. He was not trained in the arts of speech. In an oratorical contest with Cicero and Demosthenes and Daniel Webster, no doubt He would have failed to win the highest honors, if the contest were judged along conventional lines.

And yet, He was one of the greatest speakers of all time, unquestionably the greatest in the permanent effectiveness of His speaking.

No doubt the style of His speech has been obscured by the greatness of His message. We are so concerned with the truths propounded in the Sermon on the Mount that we give no thought to the delivery. The disciples recorded what He said, but they gave no account of how He said it. Probably they were so enthralled by His words that they never thought of His preaching style.

One of the greatest compliments which can be paid a speaker is for his hearers to become so absorbed in what he says that they disregard his manner of speaking. A still greater compliment is implied when the listeners go out to do the things which the speaker has advocated, even to the extent of changing their lives.

While Jesus is not listed with the great "orators," we know that He was a supremely effective speaker, and we shall do well to study His method and then follow His example in our talking.

"The common people heard Him gladly."

Why did they listen with such attention? Why did they adopt His philosophy? Why did they leave all and follow Him? The answer is found basically in the message which He had to deliver, but in addition, it is found in His way of presenting the message.

75

He spoke simply. He used plain language, the everyday language of the people.

His speech was concrete. He dealt with the most abstruse and difficult matters in terms of practical living. He led His hearers from the known to the unknown.

He made full use of illustrations, employing matters with which the people were well acquainted. The lilies of the field, the sower and the seed, the wandering sheep, the fowls of the air and many other commonplace things were brought into His speech to make the meanings clear.

He helped them to understand the most profound and mystical truths about God and about life by the use of parables, analogies, figures of speech, instead of confusing them with abstruse and incomprehensible philosophies.

He could not show them God, but He could liken God to an earthly father, or a king, or a shepherd, or a friend, and the people could understand. He was a masterful user of word pictures.

There was in His words a sense of authority. That is a great help to any speaker. The realization that the speaker knows what he is talking about makes all the difference in the world to an intelligent listener. Jesus talked about what He knew, and the people listened because there was no doubt of His knowledge and His sincerity.

And then He caused the people to think for themselves. He helped them to answer their own questions. An intelligent inquirer came to Him one day, asking, "What must I do to inherit life eternal?" Jesus replied with a question: "What is written in the law?" The man gave the right answer, and Jesus advised him to act on his own knowledge.

While we have no record of His manner of speaking, we may infer from what He said something of the way He said it.

His words give a supreme exemplification of the power of truth and calmness. They are direct, simple, plain, convincing. His style of speaking must have been like that.

It is hard, perhaps impossible, for us to think of Jesus as a ranting, roaring orator, stamping the platform, waving the arms, shouting, scolding, using the various tricks of sophisticated speakers. That is not consistent with what He said. How could He have said, "Come unto me, all ye that labor and are heavy laden, and I will give you rest," except in a quiet, winning, friendly manner?

As we celebrate once more the birth of this Galilean carpenter whose message still rings around the world, and whose words are remembered and studied and quoted more generally than the words of any other man, let us take time to read again His "speeches" as they are reported in the Gospels. Then we may see for ourselves the reason why Jesus of Nazareth is entitled to the highest place among all the speakers and orators who have ever talked in this world. Perhaps we shall be wise enough to adopt for ourselves some of the earnestness, sincerity, directness and simplicity of speech which made Him unique as a speaker, and revealed Him to us as the Prince of Peace.

(Dec. 1953, pp. 1-2)

SPEECH MANNERISMS...

Mannerisms in your speech?

Certainly you have them, but that is nothing to worry about, unless they are bad ones.

It is the little touches of personality, the so-called mannerisms, which give distinction and individuality to your speech. Your problem is to keep them from giving the wrong kind of distinction.

Your speech style is marked by attitudes of the body, movements of the hands, voice inflections, facial expressions, word usages and other characteristic matters which either help or hinder your success as a speaker. Those which help produce the right effect are good. Those which distract attention and interfere with the effectiveness are bad, and must be eliminated.

As "good" mannerisms, I include the many little personal and temperamental habits of speech and action which lend piquancy without impairing effect. A bit of accent, for instance, provided it is natural and not assumed, may put interest into the commonplace. A somewhat meticulous care in enunciation, so long as it is not too obviously pedantic, is commendable. So is a wide range in choice of words, which enables a speaker to say what he has to say in a manner not just like that of every other speaker.

On the other hand, if a speaker tries to cultivate an accent, or any other eccentricity, which does not naturally belong to him, he is guilty of a cardinal offense in mannerism, and must be stopped.

You may safely write it down as an axiom that any personal characteristic or habit which makes the speech more effective is a good mannerism, while any such characteristic which distracts attention, annoys the hearer, or in any way detracts from the effectiveness is a bad mannerism. But this definition must take into consideration the personal bias of the critic. What annoys one man may merely amuse another. This makes it hard to classify mannerisms.

While there may be differences of opinion as to "good" characteristics, there is more general agreement on the bad ones, perhaps because there are so many more of them, and because the bad impresses us more than the good.

The hands are perhaps the most obvious offenders. It is a rare privilege to listen to a speaker who uses his hands effectively as an aid to his speech. Most speakers, professional or amateur, run to one of two extremes.

Either the speaker stands with embarrassing rigidity, hands clasped behind him, or held stiffly at his side, or he becomes a wildly waving windmill type, with hands and arms performing unbelievable exploits while he talks.

The speaker who stands and talks at ease is the one who can be heard without weariness. If his posture and gestures are so graceful and so unobstrusive that no one notices them, he may be counted truly successful.

You have seen the after-dinner speaker who absent-mindedly rearranges the tableware before and during his speech, or twists his napkin into cruel shapes, or gesticulates with knife or spoon.

There is the orator who shoves his hands into his pockets, rattles his keys or his money, or fumbles with his belt or his vest until one fears a premature undressing.

Objectionable mannerisms of the hands are so numerous and so distressing that it is impossible to enumerate them, or even to classify them. Let's agree that the hands are a part of the speaker's equipment of importance second only to the voice and the face. They deserve careful treatment. Here are a few simple rules which may help:

1. Don't pocket your hands, nor handle your face.

2. Let the buttons of your clothes alone.

3. Be certain, before you rise to speak, that you are properly clad, and then exercise confidence in your clothing.

4. Keep your hands handy for use, at your sides, or behind you, but never obviously tensed, and not in the same place for too long a time.

But there are some speakers who can gesticulate objectionably even with hands tied behind them.

There is the speaker who emphasizes his points with his head. Now a bit of nodding or headshaking or grimacing is all right, but even a little of it can be too much. Don't let it become a habit.

Watch out for genuflections and body bendings. You have seen a speaker taking bending exercises while he talked, especially if he is behind a table or a chair, against which he may bend his abdomen in a manner more beneficial to his own health than to his hearers. All such movements, whether back and forth or sideways, are bad mannerisms, and to be avoided.

The position of the feet is important in any case, but far more so if the speaker stands in the open, with no table to hide him. When the orator appears at "stride stand," with feet well apart, and with the appearance of being braced in position, the audience cannot be at ease. Neither is it good to walk vigorously across the back while talking. People watch the movements instead of listening.

The easiest and more useful position for the speaker, as a general rule, is something like the "parade rest" of military drill, with one foot a little ahead of the other, and with the heel of one foot not far from the instep of the other. In this position it is difficult to rock on heels and toes, or engage in various unfortunate movements.

But mannerisms are not limited to physical posture. Many enter into speech itself.

My favorite aversion is the "grunt"—the "ah" and the "er-r" with which many speakers fill in the gaps between their words. It is a bad habit and should be broken by every speaker—even by every conversationalist.

Even good words become bad ones when excessively used. Such words weaken the effectiveness of the best speech. There is great temptation in "and." It is such an easy way to begin a sentence or a paragraph, and to string many unrelated clauses together. When you nervously double it, and say "and-and," it is terrible.

But what are you going to do about mannerisms?

The first thing is to admit that you probably have some which are not helpful. The second is to set to work to identify them. The third is to eliminate them.

To do these things, you need the help of a friendly critic, and the willingness to be helped.

Every speaker needs to be coached and criticized by some observant listener, who can detect the bad mannerisms and frankly point them out. When they have been pointed out, you must study your own speech and watch yourself.

Watch other speakers to see what makes their speech good or bad. Try to find out the secret of effective delivery by studying the best speakers. When you discover in another a weakness you would criticize unfavorably, examine yourself to see whether you may have the same fault.

In general, watch your use of hands, head, face, feet, voice and words. In these lie the dangers which wreck your speech career.

There are no absolute standards for judging speech delivery. What one man does or says may be effective for him, but if you were to imitate him, you would be a failure. Be your own best self, and shun bad habits.

Certainly you have mannerisms in your speech. It would be utterly insipid if you had not. Just be sure that the mannerisms are good ones, and you will have no reason to worry on this score.

(Nov. 1947, pp. 5-7)

GOOD DELIVERY

This meaningful phrase is not limited to our national pastime—important as it is to that game.

It applies to every phase of life. It is the result of deep thought, careful study, inspirational planning, and self-discipline as well as the follow-through.

Making a speech in loud oratorical fashion so that even the man outside the door may hear, is not necessarily good delivery unless the thought expressed "delivers the goods."

Lincoln, at Gettysburg, who spoke world-shaking truths, was derided in most national news editorials as a sorrowful figure as a President, who failed utterly to measure up to the stellar performance of Edward Everett Hale, whose delivery was unimpeachable—yet his speech struck to the hearts of thinking men and proved to the world that he could deliver the goods.

As Toastmasters we learn techniques of speech presentation which make us more capable of expressing our innermost thoughts in an effective and acceptable manner.

Perhaps even Lincoln, had he had the benefit of our self-training, would have been a more effective speaker and thus escaped much of the ridicule of his countrymen; but the stature of a man is determined by what he says in a greater degree than by how he says it.

We are fortunate, today, in having available a process of self-discovery and expression which not only teaches us to observe analytically and objectively, but to think consistently, to express ourselves clearly and succinctly and in a manner that wins our audience.

Even a pitcher must have a lot on the ball as well as superior technique to lead his league.

(May 1955, Editorial, first page)

THE DELIVERY

Repeatedly we read or hear the statement: What you say is important; how you say it is hardly less important.

Articles of trifling worth may not merit careful delivery, but that which is valuable gets most thoughtful treatment.

An advertising circular may be tossed into your car window, or dropped at your front door, but a telegram or a registered letter is handed to you in person, and you must sign the receipt for it. The importance of the matter determines the care in delivery.

Your style of speech delivery is just about as important as the facts which you are to deliver. Many a fine lecture has been ruined in effect because the lecturer did not know how to deliver.

WHAT IS DELIVERY?

Speech delivery involves both the ears and the eyes of the hearers.

The ears are conscious of the voice, its modulations, its quality, its tone and pitch.

The eyes are affected by posture, gestures, facial expression, and all the visible accompaniments of talking.

Which is more important? Your judgment must tell you. Both elements are vital in successful speech.

Splendid, inspiring thoughts can be vitiated by slovenly, careless delivery, or by annoying mannerisms, whether those mannerisms offend the eyes or the ears.

(Feb. 1956, p. 24)

DON'T BE AFRAID OF FEAR

Fear is the first enemy of the speaker during his novitiate.

Unaccustomed to facing an audience, he is instinctively afraid. Reason tells him there is nothing to fear, that no one is going to attack him, however badly he may speak. The people he addresses are friendly. They want him to do well. He is in no danger of bodily harm.

But he is afraid.

Fear of the audience results from a sense of ignorance or insufficiency. The antidote to fear is knowledge. If the novice knows that he knows his subject, he has taken the first step to the conquest of fear.

Knowledge inspires self-confidence, and knowledge plus confidence will overcome fear of the audience.

There is a great difference to be noted between fear and the nervous intensity which even the ablest speaker feels when he faces a group of people whose interest he must hold. That nervous stimulation is normal and desirable. If the speaker does not get stirred up, neither will the audience.

The kind of fear which distresses the novice is that which we

81

call "stage fright." It is readily overcome by experience and practice. The initial novelty quickly wears off, and the speaker finds himself gaining ease and confidence, becoming better poised. But this does not happen if he is not well prepared.

The unprepared speaker has a right to be scared. His own neglect imposes the fear based on ignorance.

Fear is not only the enemy of the speaker. It is the enemy of good health and well being. Whether we are speakers or not, we cannot afford to be afraid. We must not entertain the unnecessary fears which hinder and hamper us in all our activities.

Fear depresses the organic action of the body, deranges the processes of nutrition, lowers efficiency and induces disease. Carried to excess, it may weaken the will and permanently impair health.

Just as we can rout other enemies by taking proper steps, we can kill our enemy, fear. We can overcome laziness by getting to work; cowardice by self-discipline, wastefulness by the practice of thrift; and we can overcome fear by gaining knowledge.

Emile Coué wrote: "If you persuade yourself that you can do a certain thing, provided this thing be possible, you will do it, however difficult it may be. If, on the contrary, you imagine that you cannot do the simplest thing in the world, it is impossible for you to do it, and so molehills become for you unscalable mountains."

Don't be scared. Don't admit, even to yourself, that the undertaking is too hard for you. Don't dodge your chance to speak.

Remind yourself that you can think and talk as well when standing as when you are seated. Remember that your audience is just a group of individuals. You can converse easily with one or two people. It is no harder when there are several individuals listening to you. An audience of a hundred people is made up of individuals, any one of whom you can talk with individually. Talk with the group as with one person.

Let the audience be stimulating rather than alarming, and hold on to this note of encouragement: Training and practice will wear away the fear of the audience.

So start with a strong, well-defined purpose when you make a speech. Talk about what you know. Act as though you were not afraid. Cultivate the feeling of confidence. Tell yourself that you have something good to share with your audience, which both they and you can enjoy. And then keep on practicing.

Another deadly enemy of the speaker is laziness. This is the twin of fear. You can't overcome fear unless you also conquer laziness and learn to apply yourself to the task in hand.

Thinking and studying are hard work. Indolence shrinks from them.

It is reasonable, therefore, to exhort you to be afraid of being lazy—so much afraid of it that you will not yield to the temptation to neglect or postpone preparation of the speech which you are to make. Laziness and procrastination have ruined more speeches and speakers than all the fears of the audience.

We do not have to be afraid of laziness. We can master it, and when we have done that, there will be few other fears left for us to fear.

Fear of the audience is largely a state of mind. The would-be speaker ought to be able to control and direct his mental processes. He can cultivate the positive, cheerful, hopeful attitude toward life and its activities, and as he thus creates an atmosphere of optimism, he forgets his fears. He emphasizes in his own mind the importance of the message he is to give, and the pleasure his audience is to receive. Presently his fears are lost in pleasant anticipations.

Fear and indolence are the twin enemies of the speaker. Overcome fear with knowledge and indolence with endeavor. Life will become richer and finer when these two adversaries are laid low.

(Aug. 1957, pp. 23-24)

HOW DO YOU STAND?

The success of the speaker depends in some measure on the way he stands when he speaks. He should present himself well.

A sloppy, careless stance puts him at a disadvantage in two ways. First, it tends to alienate his audience. Second, it is reflected in his manner of speaking.

A good position works in the opposite way. It makes the speaker feel confidence in himself, and it attracts favorable attention from his hearers.

To stand well, the speaker should cultivate certain habits. He needs to stand erect, but without stiffness or tension. He is not "stand-offish," but rather gives the effect of approaching the audience. Without actually leaning toward them, he seems to come close to them.

He takes full advantage of his height, never seeking to conceal it by appearing to crouch or hold himself down. He stands tall.

The basis for a good position is in the placing of the feet. One of the best ways of placing them is in the military position of "parade rest." In this, he places the left foot slightly forward, with the right foot a few inches to the rear, and with the left heel pointed toward the right instep. The relative positions of the feet can be shifted occasionally, without any shuffling.

This position has the advantage of discouraging the tendency to sway from side to side, and it helps the speaker relax.

In general, the best position for the speaker is a natural, easy one, free from freakishness. He stands up, resting his weight easily on both feet. He avoids all rocking, swaying, bending and other aimless movements. He tries to stand naturally, at his best.

(Sept. 1959, p. 29)

CAN YOU READ?

Of course you can read; that is, you can read to yourself. But can you read aloud, to other people?

A great many people, some of them able speakers, seem unable to speak from a script in a satisfactory manner. They permit the script to break contact with the audience, and thus impair the effect of what they are saying.

You need look no further than your TV screen for evidence of this. Observe how speakers appear when reading from script. Note how the speaker glues his eyes to the copy which he is reading, and merely pronounces the words as though no one else were present.

Perhaps he glances up for an instant now and then, giving you the impression that he is winking at you. Perhaps he stops speaking when he looks up to see if you are still there, and so breaks the continuity.

Even some of our great political leaders are guilty of such misconduct, and some of our most experienced newscasters have the same bad habits.

Perhaps you are guilty, yourself!

Every speaker should be able to read from script without permitting it to come between him and his hearers. He should learn to look ahead in his reading, so that he can speak a sentence without looking at the script. He should be so familiar with this material that he can give the gist of it without being confined absolutely to the written or printed text. He should cultivate fluency and smoothness in his reading.

You can gain good experience by reading aloud when you are at home, or when you are alone. Practice looking ahead as you read, and see how many words or sentences you can grasp at a glance. If a member of the family will listen to you, see how much of the time

84

you can keep your eye on the auditor.

It will pay you, in your club, to undertake practice in reading. The program committee should frequently arrange for such reading practice.

And you might refer to Project Seven, in your Basic Training manual, for additional help.

(Dec. 1963, pp. 12-13)

HOW TO REMEMBER YOUR SPEECH

Since the emphasis in the Toastmasters Club is laid on extemporaneous speech, the speaker has no worry about memorizing a form of words. His training helps him develop ability to clothe his thoughts with words as he speaks.

What he has to remember is the point of his speech, and how he is to make it. This is a matter of purpose and organization.

With a definite purpose as his destination, and with a definite plan to reach that destination, all the speaker has to do is to remember his plan, his road map, his outline, and if he has prepared a natural progression from start to finish, the outline can be counted on to be remembered almost automatically.

The first thing to think about, in preparing a speech, is the last thing which the speaker will say.

That is, the conclusion of his speech—the clincher—the whip-cracker—the final appeal—must be in sight even before he figures out how to start. That is logical, for he must know where he is going before he can make the start. The destination determines the direction.

The experienced speaker, having selected the field in which his speech is to be located, immediately decides on what he intends to accomplish—on the purpose. If the purpose is not clear in his mind, he studies the subject until he is able to define his thinking, and then formulates the purpose.

Having done this, his next step is to decide how he will start the speech so as to point it toward the goal, winning the favorable attention of his audience, and leading them to think along with him.

With the opening and the closing of the speech thus definitely in mind, he constructs a pathway from the opening to the close which will get him over the route in a logical manner, within the limits of his time.

All that he needs to do now, in order to "memorize" his speech, is to travel that path mentally until he has it so clearly in mind that there is no danger of wandering or forgetting. Each thought naturally suggests the next one, because the reasoning is so logically fitted together that the points of the speech demand to be presented in order. It is like watching a motion picture, or a map, or a production line along which some mechanism moves toward completion.

How can you remember your speech?

Get the destination thoroughly in mind. Know when you are to arrive there. Construct the road by which you will travel to that destination.

If you are in earnest, if you have a sincere purpose, you need not be afraid of forgetting.

But if you do not have a clear purpose, the best plan is to forget the speech in advance.

(Oct. 1948, p. 11)

BE A DICTATOR TO YOUR MIND

Concentration is one of the lost, or nearly lost, mental powers of most Americans.

We have forgotten how to pay attention. We do not know how to listen and observe. Because we do not practice concentration, we forget names and faces and facts. We let our minds wander from the main point, and so we never catch that point.

Most of us do not understand about things because we do not pay attention. Our wits, such as they are, go wool-gathering even while we talk, and much more while others talk. Then we complain about our poor memories.

Think of the person whom you met a little while ago. You know him well, so you could speak his name and exchange the usual inane greetings. But beyond that, what was said? Can you remember what kind of clothes he was wearing? Did he have a necktie, or was he wearing a sport shirt? Did he wear a hat, or was he sunning his roof?

Try to mention someone you have met. His name escapes you. You speak of him as "whatcha-may-call-him" or "that guy down in the real estate office" or "Bill—oh, you know him as well as I do, but I just can't recall his name."

Perhaps you are working in the garden, and you need another tool. You shout to the small son, "Jimmy, will you bring me that gadget out of the garage—that thingumabob that I use to tighten that what's-it?" With a moment's thought, you could remember the name of the monkey wrench or the alligator wrench or the garden fork, or whatever it is that you need. The trouble is that we talk so often without thinking.

Some jingler has written:

They never taste who always drink;

They always talk who never think.

You positively can control your mind, but it takes effort and will power to do it. Conditions around us conspire to distract attention and make concentration harder, but you can do it if you will.

We listen to the radio while reading the newspaper, or while driving the car. But we are not really listening. Our attention is divided. When we get through we cannot remember either the headlines or the radio program. We might better turn off the radio or lay aside the paper. Our minds are not capable of concentrating on two things at once. We have to keep our minds on what we are doing.

This failure of attention drives advertisers crazy, and in turn, their product tends to increase our inattention. They know that a billboard will not register with the passing public unless it has an eye-catcher, like something in motion. Thus we see animated billboards, with a washerwoman elbow deep in suds, or a puddlejumping car, or a mule doing a high kick. Even in the newspaper, the type is so big that it fairly screams at you, or you do not notice the ad.

It is a reflection of the times in which we live. We are constantly assailed by so many noises and sights that we become confused, calloused, inattentive in self-defense.

But if we are going to produce results of any merit, we must exert our mental strength to rise above these distractions. We can shut out the noises when we become engrossed in some line of thought. We can ignore our surroundings as we listen to some speaker of worth. We can even improve our memories if we learn to concentrate.

Concentration and frequent review are the twin keys to better memory and better thinking. We can disregard unimportant things, and fix attention on that which matters most. Then we can bring back in review the things we wish to retain. By that process we can remember names and faces, or speech outlines, or important engagements and errands.

It is not easy, but it is possible. You can control your thoughts, and you can build a dependable memory, but you can't do it by merely wishing for it. If it is worth your while, you will accomplish it by

concentrated persistent effort. You must be a dictator to your mind!
(July 1954, pp. 3-4)

"THROW AWAY YOUR NOTES"

This is a bit of advice heard all too frequently from an evaluator in a Toastmasters Club. It is not good advice, however well intended.

The use of notes is a skill which every speaker should cultivate. It is true that there is greater freedom when one speaks without reference to anything but his audience, but it is equally true that the speaker often needs the safety and reassurance given by having before him some materials with which to refresh his memory.

Use small cards for your notes. The three by five inch size is good, and even a slightly smaller card will serve. Place only a few words on each card—just enough to help your memory. Key words or phrases will remind you of the point which comes next. These should be written or typed in letters large enough to read without close scrutiny. If the cards must be held in the hand, hold them unobtrusively, and lay them down on the table except when you need them.

Never hold the cards in your hand while gesturing. Do not wave them at your audience. Do not permit them to interfere with eye contact.

Notes are a support, an insurance to the speaker. They help to keep him from forgetting or digressing. But they are good only when properly used.

Don't throw them away. Learn to use them, by careful practice, and then when you need them, they will be a help and not a hindrance.
(March 1960, pp. 28-29)

SPEAKING AT-TO-WITH

Each of these words describes an attitude of the speaker.

You have heard and watched speakers in all three poses. Which do you prefer?

When you speak, no doubt you assume one of the three attitudes. Do you know which one it is? Do you believe that it is the best and most effective one for you?

AT—

This speaker talks away from his audience. His characteristic position for speaking is with arms folded, or standing sidewise. If reading, he keeps his eyes glued to the script. He avoids direct contact with his audience. He keeps them at arm's length, or beyond. He permits no familiarity. He maintains his dignity. Rarely, if ever, does he unbend. He talks at the people.

His dogmatic, didactic or aloof attitude may be unintentional and even unconscious to him, but it sets a barrier between him and his audience. No matter what pearls of wisdom or flashes of eloquence may fall from his lips, his attitude creates a sense of distance which does not lend enchantment. He does not "get next" to his hearers.

TO—

Much easier to follow is the speaker who talks to his audience. He may fail to establish any sense of intimacy, and he does not develop a good eye contact, although he is not nearly so far away from them as the "at" speaker. He may speak in a dictatorial tone. He may give orders by his manners, but at least he stays in the same room with his hearers.

Many preachers and a large number of teachers and other professional people are afflicted with this style of speech. Their material may be excellent and full of interest, in which case the people who listen forget the resentment aroused by the attitude of talking down to them, or of giving orders, but they can never get on to the level of friendship which is essential between teacher and pupil, and between speaker and audience.

Sometimes, after you have listened to a preacher or a teacher who talks "to" his hearers, you have met him off the platform and have been amazed and charmed by his friendly personality. Perhaps you have wished that he would carry his genial, winning manner with him when he mounts the podium.

Once more, analyze your own speech, and ask your critics to tell you about your own manner. Do you have a tendency to get away from your audience, and talk to them?

WITH—

Occasionally you find a speaker who does not talk at you nor to you. He gives you the impression that he is talking with you, and what he says is directed to your ears and your mind, just as truly as though he were sitting beside you while speaking.

There is nothing distant nor impersonal in this man's speech. The warmth of his disposition pervades his words and gives them unobstructed entry into your thinking. Even if you are in disagreement, he does not arouse active opposition.

One of the great examples of this kind of speaker is found in Franklin D. Roosevelt, who could deliver a speech on the radio in such a way that you felt as though he were sitting in the living room with you, and talking to you and your family alone. His way of speaking won friends even among those who were politically opposed.

Will Rogers was another example of the same thing. When you heard him deliver a "lecture" you had the feeling that this was just good old Will, and that he was talking things over with you. He would like to hear your opinion if there were time for it.

The ability to approach an audience in that friendly style is partly a gift of nature, and partly a cultivated art. It is worth cultivating if you want to be as effective as possible in your speech. The sympathetic, understanding, friendly attitude on the platform awakens in the audience a similar reaction, which is a great help to the speaker.

BUT BE CAREFUL

Don't overdo it.

Don't sacrifice your dignity for the sake of being a "common" person. Don't lose your authority while talking things over.

There is a rare and most desirable skill to be attained by the good speaker, in establishing and maintaining the right attitude of mutual sympathy, friendship and respect between himself and his audience. This is something for which every speaker must strive as he reaches out for improvement in speaking.

Evaluation will help. Your evaluators can tell you what you lack in your approach to your hearers, and if you are wise, you will apply their opinions to your talking. The improvement will be worth all the effort it takes.

For effective speaking, try to talk with your audience.

(Jan. 1954, pp. 7-8)

Evaluation—
Constructive Criticism

Evaluation of both speaking and club conduct was considered by Dr. Smedley to be vital in Toastmasters. His writings in this area show his point of view quite clearly but also the tendency of many to misunderstand him. An article which appeared in 1945 indicates that he was not entirely pleased that his comments on criticism had been taken quite literally by many.

MEA CULPA

Yes, it is my fault. I'll take the blame.

But from this day through all time to come, I disclaim further responsibility, and refuse to accept the blame, or the credit.

In my earlier days as a teacher of public speaking I was inclined to be dogmatic. I emphasized my personal likes and dislikes, and made rules to fit. If I did not like some mannerism or form of speech, I said it was wrong and must never be done. If I liked it, I gave it an approved rating.

Then I accepted these *dicta* as rules of speech, and taught as though they were. To this day we hear it said of certain mannerisms, "A Toastmaster never does that." And I realize that the critic speaker is quoting my misguided statements of long ago. Thus, it is my fault.

I disliked apologies from the speaker—meaningless movements— hands in pockets—all sorts of things—and I said, "A good speaker—a Toastmaster—never apologizes," or "pockets his hands," or whatever the case might be.

What I really meant was, "I don't like for a speaker to do that. It bothers me—distracts my attention."

I forgot that I was just one member of the audience, and that other people might like what distressed me. I took my own ideas too seriously.

As a result, one hears the remark all too often even today, that "A Toastmaster never apologizes."

Frankly, that isn't so, any more than that a good speaker never puts his hands in his pockets.

There are occasions when it is not only desirable but necessary for a speaker to make an explanation, which might be construed as an apology. There are situations in which hands in the pockets are quite in order. There are conditions to justify almost any mannerism or gesture of which man is capable.

It is when a mannerism or action becomes habitual, and is in itself a hindrance to the effect of the speech that it becomes objectionable. There is no rule by which one can state that a certain mannerism is always bad. Circumstances always modify rules.

Having made my confession and washed my hands of responsibility for the captious critic who chirps, "A good Toastmaster never apologizes," let me speak this word of caution:

While no gesture nor mannerism may be classed as bad, *per se,* it is safe to say that any such action is bad if it detracts from the effectiveness of the speech. Anything which keeps the speaker from making his point, from winning the vote, from convincing his audience, is bad practice and should be discontinued. Anything which strengthens his speech and helps him to make the sale to his audience is good enough to use, but must be used only when needed. Beyond this, let no one try to lay down general rules for the speaker which will cover all specific cases.

It is always the speaker's responsibility to make his speech effective. If he does that, applaud him; commend him; vote for him, even though he violates all the rules in the book. If he doesn't put it over, even though he follows every rule, his speech is not a success. The test of the speech is not in following the textbook, but in making the sale.

(Sept. 1945, pp, 4-5)

EVALUATION—THE PERVASIVE PRINCIPLE

Evaluation—criticism—appraisal—discrimination—whatever you prefer to call it, is at the very foundation of all human progress. In no part of your life can you escape it, or keep from using it.

The ability to evaluate objects, conditions, thoughts, ideas, is the human characteristic which brought primitive man out of his caves and trees, and set him on the road to civilized living. The same talent helps him today to reach higher standards of life and to achieve better things for himself and his fellows.

You use the faculty every time you make a choice, for you must evaluate in order to choose. Freedom of choice implies freedom to criticize.

However eloquent the speaker may be, his training is unbalanced unless it enables him to evaluate speeches fairly, intelligently and constructively. Intelligent listening is as important as effective speaking.

No Toastmasters Club is fulfilling its obligation to its members unless it brings them the maximum of training in the art of constructive criticism.

(Sept. 1952, pp. 1-2)

Dr. Smedley's understanding of the classical concepts of rhetoric and public speaking gave him an independence of thought and willingness to challenge the philosophy of any writer whose approach varied markedly from that which he found to be effective through application in Toastmasters. For example, he compares the critical attitude of Cato, whose criticisms Cicero considered to be "harsh and inelegant," to that of the Toastmasters evaluator:

WHAT A TOASTMASTER
HE WOULD HAVE MADE

Marcus Porcius Cato—"Cato the Censor"— Born 234 B.C. A farmer who went into war and politics, and who won the credit for laying the foundations of Latin literature.

Cato, on observing that statues were being set up in honor of many, remarked: "I would rather people would ask why is there not a statute to Cato than why there is."

He was a man of strong convictions and powerful prejudices. He was an outspoken, two-fisted hater. I am not so certain that he would have been a good Toastmaster, after all.

Cato the Censor would have been a powerful critic in our clubs, assuming that we count criticism to be fault-finding. How he would have enjoyed "giving the speaker the works," "tearing the speech apart," "burning up the speaker!"

Perhaps the times required a man of this type. Possibly no one less vigorous could have won recognition as the founder and former of Latin prose.

He did not start out to be a literary figure. In fact, he wrote to decry writing, and especially to discredit the Greek style, which was no less than violent poison to him.

There is not much of Cato's writings left to us now. We owe most of our knowledge of him to Plutarch and Cicero and other notables who lived with and after him, who appreciated his ability in spite of his disposition. The only one of his writings which survives is a treatise on farming.

Yes, he was a farmer. He became a soldier when circumstances required fighting. Then he went on to be a lawyer, rising in due time to the eminence of such posts as *quaestor, aedile, praetor,* and finally, *consul* and *censor.*

Cato loved strife, and his long life was a series of combats, verbal and otherwise.

He hated many things, but as his extra special, Number One hate he classed the Greek literature and the Greek people and everything that was Greek. You could safely call him a Hellenophobiac. And he didn't like Carthage or the Carthaginians, either, as we observed in his oft-repeated slogan: "Carthage must be destroyed."

He really was not an amiable man, but how he could talk! Even those things which he approved were harshly treated, and those he disliked were excoriated. Someone has said of him that even virtue did not present itself to Cato in an amiable form. In many respects, he reminds us of some political leaders in our day, such as—well, let's not name any names.

In a Toastmasters Club of today, he would hardly know how to accept criticism gracefully, and he certainly would not be able to give it with tact. Can you imagine a speech evaluator telling Cato to drape his toga more gracefully, or to put a smile into his speech?

He was so dead sure that he was right, and so determined to prevail over opposition, that he could forget all the rules of speech, if he knew any, in his headlong rush to overthrow his opponents.

Conviction, combativeness and enthusiasm were his trademarks. His style of speech, according to those who knew him, was "rude, unpolished, ungraceful, but always convincing." "His statements were clear, his arguments direct, his illustrations striking, his epithets appropriate, and his wit keen." He was a master of satire, and used it ruthlessly. He thought himself above "art" and when he got under way, the finer points of grammar and rhetoric had to look out for themselves. He never hesitated to call a spade a spade, or even worse.

Cato was a formidable accuser and just as powerful a defender. "He spoke as if in hand to hand conflict with an adversary." He pushed out his arguments with force, brevity and sense, and with a very mean disposition.

Austere, unamiable, self-centered, his character gave rise to the epigram that he was so morose and disagreeable that Persephone herself would not receive him into the infernal regions.

You might compare that with the remark credited to Father Taylor, who said, when speaking of a great American, so different in personality from Cato, and yet a notable leader: "If Emerson goes to hell, he will start a wave of emigration in that direction."

Let's give Cato full credit for his ability; honor him for his amazing versatility and variety of talent; recognize his achievement in those early days of Rome, on battlefield and on the rostrum; but if you want to maintain peace and harmony in your club, don't invite Cato the Censor, or any spiritual descendant of his to become a member.

(March 1946, pp. 14-15)

One of Dr. Smedley's best and most definite statements of his philosophy was written four years later. This and the articles which follow in this section have been selected primarily because they express the man rather than because they give details and the mechanics for speech criticism. His "how to" publication, Speech Evaluation, *implements the philosophy presented here.*

CONSTRUCTIVE CRITICISM
IS ONE OF THE FINE ARTS

Criticism is an art, although it has never been listed as one of the fine arts. On the contrary, it has usually been directed toward or against the so-called fine arts of music, poetry, painting, drama, and the like.

Speech evaluation is a branch of this art, but in purposes and methods it is radically different from what is generally recognized as literary or art or dramatic criticism. Our definition of criticism may be stated: "A process of evaluation and appraisal for the purpose of improvement."

This is constructive criticism, as practiced in the Toastmasters Clubs. It is not merely a matter of pointing out faults without suggestions for improvement, but it is a definite technique for promoting better work through identification of faults and suggestion of means for correcting them.

Fault-finding without suggestions for improvement is a waste of time.

In the Toastmasters Club, no worthy critic ever uses his opportunity to show off his cleverness at the expense of the speaker, nor takes the occasion to air his prejudices and personal idiosyncrasies. On the contrary, he undertakes to reflect for the speaker the reaction of the audience, so that strong points may be emphasized and encouraged, and weaknesses may be eliminated.

Standards of criticism are difficult to determine. This is true in all the arts. As a rule, the standards are set by the individual critic, on the basis of his personal likes and dislikes and prejudices. The critic looks at a picture, reads a book, listens to music, and he either likes it or dislikes it. If he likes it, he pronounces it good. If it displeases him, he condemns it. Sometimes he seems to enjoy being displeased, so that he can show off his cleverness.

In mathematics or the sciences, there are exact standards. A problem is correctly solved, or it is not. There are rules by which to evaluate and establish the grades. This is not the case in the performance of the artist, whose work is judged by its effect.

There is the true standard for the speech evaluator. The final test of a speech is the results it accomplishes.

The speech evaluator must everlastingly keep before him five vital questions, as he listens with analytical mind.

First, what did the speaker intend to accomplish by his speech?

Second, what did he actually accomplish?

Third, what elements in his speech (material, construction, delivery) helped him to gain the desired result?

Fourth, what elements in his speech hindered his accomplishment?

Fifth, what does he need to do in order to make his next speech better?

Even so, it must be remembered that the evaluator expresses his own personal reaction. Others may have reacted differently. It is good for the speaker to have more than one evaluator, for this reason, so that diversity of opinion may be expressed.

There are occasions when some member, not fully in accord with what the evaluator has said, should ask the privilege of stating his opinion on some point of difference.

There are occasions when the speaker himself should be given liberty to question his evaluator on any point which is not clear.

All these matters must be handled with tact, courtesy and sincerity. Speaker and evaluator must recognize their mutual obligation to evaluate tactfully and helpfully, and to accept criticism gracefully and with appreciation.

Completely out of place in the Toastmasters Club is any suggestion that the critic should "tear the speech apart," or "burn up the speaker," or "give him the works." Instead, let the critic show how to put the speech together; how to build up the speaker; how to give him help he needs.

For any man to qualify himself as a thoroughly good evaluator, there is required much analytical listening, much study of speeches and speakers, and much self-examination as to why he reacts to certain ways.

One of the finest things about this part of Toastmasters training is the fact that the good evaluator gains immeasurably for himself in learning how to deal with other people; how to give advice and suggestions without offending; and how to judge and appraise men in all sorts of situations—not merely as public speakers.

Still better, experience as an evaluator of speech develops the attitude of helpful interest in others, and teaches the evaluator to be tolerant, even with those who disagree with him.

The privilege of serving as an evaluator or critic is one of the choicest advantages of membership in a Toastmasters Club. No member can afford to miss his chance to listen, appraise, and suggest improvements. Better skip your speech assignment than miss out on the appointment as evaluator.

Whatever your situation as to other fine arts, you have an opportunity to make yourself adept in the art of criticism by your participation in the work of speech evaluation as a member of the Toastmasters Club.

Rightly used and directed, constructive criticism is one of the finest of all the arts known to man. It is fundamental to the development of all the others.

(Sept. 1949, pp. 1-2)

CAN YOU TAKE IT?

Every Toastmaster learns, early in his membership, that one of the fundamental purposes of his training is to promote, for him, the technique of tactfully giving and gracefully receiving criticism, and profiting thereby. The man who learns this great lesson builds into his personality something of incalculable value to him, entirely apart from what it does for his improvement in speech.

The practice of friendly criticism, or "speech evaluation" is an essential in every Toastmasters Club.

WHAT IT IS

Speech evaluation, constructive criticism, appraisal—call it what you will—boils down to just one thing: getting the audience reaction to a speech, and letting the speaker know about it in a way that will help him to do better.

Criticism does not necessarily mean fault-finding. It may just as properly mean praise, or commendation, or appreciation. "Neither praise nor blame is the object of true criticism. Justly to discriminate, wisely to prescribe, and honestly to award—these are the true aims and duties of criticism."

Speech evaluation, as practiced in the Toastmasters Club, is a process of revealing to the speaker the extent to which his speech has achieved its purpose, convinced his audience, made the "sale," with the reasons on which the evaluator bases his judgments. Such helpful criticism is always friendly in tone—never harsh, biting, discouraging, sarcastic.

Consider this: When you go to see your dentist, you ask him to criticize your teeth. He probes around to find weaknesses. The probing may hurt, but the hurt is in your jaw, not in your mind. He finds the good teeth and says, "O.K." He finds the cavities and says, "These must be repaired." That is a good example of the work of a faithful speech evaluator. Don't be hurt if he finds fault. But you may feel relieved and encouraged when he says, "O.K. on that point."

WHY WE USE IT

An experienced speaker may be able to sense the reaction of his hearers by the degree of attention they give him, or by their response to his appeal, but even he may have a hard time finding out just why they reacted as they did.

The inexperienced speaker cannot hope to understand this reaction unless someone tells him about it. He knows that all who listen are criticizing him inwardly, silently, as he speaks, but he gets no good from them unless some of them speak out and frankly tell him.

Every speaker needs frequently to test his ability by means of frank, friendly, spoken comments by those who hear him.

Every speaker, even the best, unconsciously falls into bad habits of speech which he may never discover by himself.

The speaker who is honestly trying to make himself a better speaker welcomes the helpful comments and honest expressions of his hearers who listen intelligently and critically.

In turn, he serves as a critic for his fellow Toastmasters, and thus he develops the habit of analytical listening. By pointing out the good points and the bad ones in the speeches he hears, he discovers his own needs for improvement. He turns his criticisms on himself.

Thus, by criticizing and being criticized, he gains understanding and facility.

HOW WE USE IT

The Toastmasters Clubs have pioneered in the practice of evaluation by members of the audience rather than by expert or professional critics and teachers of speech. Results have justified this experiment.

Criticism of a speech by an ordinary citizen, not skilled in the technicalities of public speaking, is less systematic and scientific than that given by an expert, but it has the advantage of reflecting the views and reactions of the common listener, to whom the speech is directed.

It has the further advantage of training the listener to listen critically, analytically, and it will help him to identify his own faults and to correct them as he studies the weaknesses of others.

In the typical Toastmasters Club meeting, each speech given on the formal program is briefly evaluated by a member-critic, appointed to evaluate that speech, while the entire meeting, including the critics, is reviewed by a general critic, usually one of the more experienced members.

The simplest formula for speech evaluation can be stated thus:

What did I like best about the speech?

What features in the speech or its delivery did not appeal to me?

Did the speaker have a purpose, and did he make good on it?

What definite thing should he do to improve himself in speech?

Did he "make a sale" to me?

(Aug. 1964, pp. 14-15)

SPEECH EVALUATION

In a program which includes 'five short speeches, the standard plan is to assign one man as critic for each speaker. Each critic is given a specific time, usually not in excess of two minutes, for his critical remarks. He is advised to limit his criticism to certain features, and to make his comments in the form of a very short, but well considered speech.

The "General Critic," or "Master Evaluator," or "Evalumaster," as he is variously called, has general charge of the work of criticism for the evening. He may direct the form to be followed and make special assignments to the individual critics. When his turn comes to offer comments, he covers the conduct of the entire meeting, but does not go over the comments given by the individual critics, except to correct errors which they may have made.

Criticism must be timed as carefully as the speeches. If it becomes careless, stilted, unvaried in form, too much standardized or too careless of time values, it can be a hindrance, even a nuisance.

HOW TO GIVE CRITICISM

There is just one purpose fundamental to the use of criticism in a Toastmasters Club. That purpose is to help the speaker to improve himself.

A speaker is helped by three lines of comment.

First, his strong points are emphasized, and second, his weaknesses and faults are pointed out. The inevitable result is seen in suggestions for improvement. These three fundamentals should underlie every criticism.

All criticism or evaluation given in a Toastmasters Club is friendly, constructive and helpful. It should reflect the honest reactions of the critic, given without any suggestion of unpleasantness or fault-finding. Harsh, unkindly, sarcastic criticism will defeat the whole purpose and create lasting animosities.

HOW TO TAKE CRITICISM

Listen attentively to your critic. Try to learn everything possible from him. Cultivate the attitude of appreciative reception. Keep all feelings of resentment or opposition from your mind. Make notes of suggestions offered.

But remember that the critic expresses only his own opinion. If you can get reactions from several listeners, these are better than one man's opinion, and among them you will get the greater help.

Accept all criticisms either in the club or outside, with thanks and honest appreciation. Cultivate the open mind. Even if the critic is unfriendly, he may help you. Ability to take criticism gracefully and apply it effectively is one of the marks of a truly great man.

RESULTS FROM THE CRITICISM

What values may you, as a member, expect to gain from criticism?

Why submit yourself to this embarrassing, perhaps distressing experience?

You need to know how you impress people—how they react to you. Perhaps some very small mannerisms or habits of speech are hindering you. Possibly these same habits keep you from making the best impression on people you meet. By correcting them you may be able to change your ways for the better.

The critic holds up the mirror for you. He reflects the impression you have made on him. If you don't like the reflection, you should take the hint to improve it. The critic is not responsible for your speech. He merely tells you how he heard it and how it impressed him. Thank him for being honest, and then be as honest in using his suggestions.

You should make perceptible growth in character and personality from giving and receiving critical comments.

You will learn how to get along with other people—how to make yourself acceptable among your fellows.

When your faults are pointed out, try to correct them. The story is told of a man who took a position as clerk in a store. After a week, the proprietor said to him, "What experience did you say you have had in the grocery business?" "I have had ten years of experience," replied the clerk, with pride. "Well, sir," said the proprietor, "it appears to me that you just spent ten years practicing your mistakes." A wise speaker does not "practice" his mistakes. He corrects them.

Criticism is the common denominator of Toastmasters. We are not experts. Every man speaks his own mind and every man learns from every other one. The newest member may give a helpful suggestion to an experienced speaker, and vice versa. The spirit of helpfulness is characteristic of Toastmasters. Each wishes to help the others. Through the exchange of ideas in speech evaluation, we help, even as we wish to be helped.

(Sept. 1964, pp. 10-11)

THE SPEAKER WANTS TO KNOW

There are four things which every speaker needs to know about his speech, as the audience heard it. To give him information on these points is the purpose of evaluation as practiced in the Toastmasters Club.

First, the speaker would like to know what was good about his speech. How did it sound to the listeners? How did he, the speaker, look to them? The evaluator has the chance right here to sprinkle a bit of sugar where it will do the most good. He may have to apply some salt or vinegar also, but he should not overdo this.

Second, he needs to know (although he may not be eager to hear it) just what was not so good about the speech. Was there trouble with his material, as to organization, logic, phrasing, or otherwise? Did undesirable mannerisms appear, either visible or audible? How did he sound to the listener, and how did he look?

Third, and this is very important, did he accomplish his purpose? Did he make that purpose clear, and did he achieve it? Did he stir the audience to action, or add to their information, or win their votes, or entertain them? The accomplishment of purpose is the fundamental test of the speech. He needs to be told frankly that he did or did not do this.

Fourth, the speaker definitely wants some suggestions for improvement. Here the evaluator has the chance to give a pat on the back, and perhaps a little push forward. Tell him how he can make his next speech more enjoyable and acceptable to you, individually and personally.

Use these four points the next time you act as evaluator, and see how much good advice you can give in a few words, to help the speaker in his effort to do better. Imagine that he is asking you the questions. He says:

1. What, if anything, was good about my speech?

2. What was unsatisfactory about my speech, in your judgment?

3. Did I get the point across? Did I accomplish my purpose?

4. What do you suggest by way of helping me to improve?

THE SPEAKER CAN FIND OUT

You, as his evaluator, will tell him what he wants to know. In a short, snappy little speech, you may say something like this: "I especially liked your speech because you had a purpose. You made the purpose clear at the start, and you emphasized it in your conclusion. You really sold me on the proposition. But I did not like the way you stood, shuffling your feet, nor the way you used your voice, which was harsh and unappealing. Your speech content was better than your delivery.

"For improvement, I advise you to put a friendly note into your voice. Don't scold. Stand on both feet, using your full stature, and occasionally bring one or two hands out of exile and let them have a part in the speech.

"There are some other things you need to work on, including organization of material, but these are the most obvious ones to me. Correct yourself on these points, and then we will tackle the others."

Almost any speaker will appreciate and profit by evaluation such as this. You would like it yourself.

(Feb. 1959, pp. 9-10)

CRITICISM—IS NOT FAULTFINDING

It is easy to find fault. Many people seem to enjoy doing it. Unfortunately, criticism has taken on the meaning of faultfinding in the popular usage. When we say that one has a critical attitude, we usually mean that he is a finder of faults.

That is not the true meaning of criticism, of course. The real critic is the one who appraises, evaluates, adjudicates, reviews, discriminates and seeks to arrive at the true value. He is as eager to recognize merit as to discover faults, and he distributes praise as generously as blame.

The faultfinding critic likes to call himself a realist, but all too frequently he is a pessimist. One of his trademarks is "Yes—but..."

You greet him with "This is a fine morning! See how bright the sunshine is!" He comes back with "Yes, but it won't last. See those clouds on the horizon?"

He looks at a picture, or glances through a book. You remark, "I like that one. Don't you?" He responds "Yes, but..."

That is his approach to the people about him. He may mildly like some person, but there is always something wrong to which he must call attention.

You say, "I find Bronsburger a most inspiring talker. He always gives me a lift." Your critic friend replies, "Yes, but he'll bore you to death if you don't get away from him."

You may remark, "That new man out in the shop certainly does turn out a lot of good work at his machine. He is a good worker." The old realist growls, "Yes, but did you notice how he watches the clock?"

This is not true criticism, whether it be directed at a work of art, a person, or a speech. Real criticism seeks to discover the true worth. It may point out a fault if that is serious, but it is more concerned with the final value than with the unimportant details. It welcomes the chance to commend what is commendable.

Apply this principle to speech evaluation. Apply it to your own speeches. Consider which helps you more, the evaluator who says, "I can't find much in that speech to criticize," or the one who tells you "That was a good speech, and this is what made it good for me..." and then he tells you the points of merit and suggests how you can build up your style so as to take advantage of your best features.

The good critic seeks to build up, not to tear down. He knows that by emphasizing the positive, the good things in the speech, he can lead his subject to lay aside minor faults without ever realizing that he possessed them.

A real critic never says "I can't find anything to criticize." He knows that results are what count, and that if the speech, book or picture achieved its purpose, conveyed its message, won the point, it is to be judged by that rather than by unimportant details.

In all our contacts with people and events and things, we are forced to exercise our right to discriminate and evaluate. This may involve some recognition of faults, but far better, it calls for appreciation of virtues, and it offers encouragement to the person criticized by showing him how to build on what he has.

A speaker may be too conscious of his height. He feels every inch of his six feet, and is inclined to stoop so as to reduce his stature. Commend him on his ability to make an impressive appearance, and urge him to "stand tall" so as to take full advantage of his procerity. Don't scold him for being stoop-shouldered, or for lounging as he talks.

Perhaps the speaker on whom you are working has an excellent voice, resonant and deep-toned, but his organization of material is poor. Don't romp all over him about being disorganized in his thought. Praise his voice, and tell him that he must bring the rest of his talking up to that grade of excellence. So fine a voice quality deserves to be used on the best of material.

The approach of commendation takes away the sting of your adverse criticism. When you point out the natural advantages, the speaker is more willing to accept your suggestions for improvement in other matters. You do not need to be negative.

Instead of saying, "Your grammar is deplorable," or "Your delivery is monotonous—no voice gestures, no hand gestures," or "Your hesitancy, your constant grunting, your uncertainty all make it hard to listen to you," tell him, "Practice thinking out in advance just what you want to say, and just what you must accomplish, and then get filled up with enthusiasm for the subject, and turn yourself loose. Your little mannerisms will disappear when you are really in earnest."

In a word, "accentuate the positive." When you are a critic, as you must be every hour of your day, watch for the good things and emphasize them, remembering that cultivation and encouragement will do as much for a man as for a plant in your garden.

It was well said by Joseph Addison: "A true critic ought rather to dwell upon excellences than imperfections, to discern the concealed beauties of a writer, and to communicate to the world such things as are worth their observation."

(June 1956, pp. 4-5)

JUST A LITTLE BIT

Perhaps it is because the evaluator wishes to soften his criticism and to keep from offending the speaker whom he evaluates, but it seems to me that there is altogether too much of this "just a little bit more" in our evaluation. Many of us are too timid or reticent to say what should be said. Thus we fail to give our hearers the help they need.

Suppose an evaluator says to you, "You could have been just a little more forceful in your conclusion," or "Your introduction could have been more interesting," or "You spoke a little too rapidly. Try to slow down just a little." Honestly, what good do you get from such a comment?

Conversely, when you offer such suggestions to the speaker you are evaluating, are you giving him any real help? He knows, as we all do, that "the speech could have been a little more vigorous, or better organized, or more vigorously delivered." But should it have been, and if so, why not tell him so?

I am not advocating severe or offensive criticism, but I am protesting against this mincing of words. If the speaker's speech was not well organized, or if the introduction or the conclusion was weak, you will do him a favor by saying so, in plain but friendly words; and you can help still further by giving him some example of what you mean. Tell him how to do better next time, but do not forget to speak a word of appreciation for what he did this time.

Just be a "little more careful" about your listening, and be "a little more definite" in your suggestions for improvement. It is not your business as a critic either to condemn or to praise, but when you observe bad features in the speaker's work, it is your duty to call attention to them, with suggestions for improvement; and when you note points of excellence in material or delivery, it is your privilege to mention these with approval and with encouragement.

When you evaluate, be frank, friendly, helpful, always seeking to show the way to better things, but please eliminate the phrase "just a little more" of whatever is needed. Probably you would be nearer the truth if you called for "a lot more."

WHY EVALUATE?

Why do we place so much emphasis on evaluation in our club work? What good does it do? Is it worthwhile?

Answering the first question, we may say that we emphasize this feature because it is important. When it is well done, it gives the speaker an understanding of how his speech impressed the listeners. The most important thing for a speaker to find out, whether he is a novice or an experienced talker, is the reaction of his audience. He gets this from frank and friendly criticism, and he builds on it in future speeches.

Evaluation does a vast amount of good, if it is well given, and if it is is well received. It is one of the most worthwhile activities in the Toastmasters Club—provided it is carefully and thoughtfully done.

In many of our clubs, evaluation, or constructive criticism, is the weakest part of the work. The members are not properly guided in their critical listening, because the officers and leaders fail to realize the need for such help. Thus the members who evaluate fail to get the real benefit which they should receive because the evaluators do not provide them with the kind of suggestions which they need.

Let us take a close look at just what the speaker needs from his listener. Consider your own speeches. What are the most important facts which you would like to hear discussed by your evaluator? Are you greatly helped by being told that you need "a little more force" or that you let one hand get into your pocket, or that you shifted from one foot to the other? Are such things the important items to you?

You will answer in the negative, quite naturally, for if you are a thoughtful, sincere talker, with a real message to deliver, the vital question in your mind is whether you made your point, accomplished your purpose, stimulated your hearers, gave them something to remember.

Another item which frequently troubles the speaker is the diversity of reactions—the different ways in which people hear the speech.

Suppose you have two evaluators when you give your speech. One of them says that the material was well organized, logically arranged, and that the conclusion tied in with the opening and was conclusive. The other says that your opening was weak, that it did not lead into the subject, and that your treatment did not clarify your purpose. He thought your talk was scattered, and that the ending was inconclusive.

How are you to deal with such evaluation? What good can you get from it?

The first thing to consider is that people hear with different ears. You must try to adapt your next speech so as to make your meaning clear to men of various types of mind. One hearer may be watching for points on which to disagree; another may have his own ideas on the subject, and if you do not express similar ideas, he may think you failed. Perhaps the title of your speech led him to expect a certain treatment, and certain facts to be presented, which you did not introduce.

What should you do about this? Sorry, but I can't give you a universal prescription. Above all, do not let it discourage you. Take it rather as a challenge. Try to find ways to make yourself more clearly understood next time. Recognize the difference in listening habits, and build future speeches with this in mind.

I venture to recommend a careful study of the little book entitled "Speech Evaluation," which I wrote a good many years ago, and which seems to have been quite helpful to many men. Try to understand the what and why and how of evaluation, first for your own good, and then for the sake of the help you can give to others by careful, analytical listening.

YOUR MIND ON PARADE

"Every time you speak, your mind is on parade."

I do not know who wrote that statement, but it is a sobering thought, and one with which I heartily agree. If more of us realized its meaning and its importance to us, our talking would be more carefully done. "Out of the abundance of the heart, the mouth speaketh" is another statement of the same truth, found in the Bible.

The point is that our words reveal what is in our minds. If we are thinking fine, worthy thoughts, this will be reflected in what we say, whether in ordinary conversation or in formal speeches. We need to be careful that the revelations thus made do not cost us too heavily with those who hear us.

There is the story of a man, carrying a camera, who joined a company of his acquaintances and told them: "I am going to take a picture of you. My camera is different. It does not show your outward appearance, but it gets a picture of your thoughts. It will show just what you are thinking."

There was not a man in the crowd who would stand for such a picture. All of them got away as fast as possible. They were unwilling to have their thoughts revealed to those about them.

FOR BETTER EVALUATION

The "Point of Emphasis" for September is better evaluation. There is hardly any other feature of our work which is more in need of emphasis. This time, try some variety in your club's evaluation, and present two or three well-prepared talks on the subject.

Here is a form or plan for evaluation which works well. Let your club try it a few times.

Each evaluator, and each member, for that matter, will listen to each speech with certain questions in mind. Here they are:

1. The openings. Was the speech started in an interesting manner? Did it catch your attention? Did it indicate the purpose of the speech?

2. The conclusions. In each case, was there a definite conclusion? Did it indicate what the speaker wanted you to do about it?

3. Material. Was the material well selected and arranged? Did it lead to a definite climax, or a clear conclusion?

4. Delivery. Was the speech well-delivered? What feature detracted from the effectiveness?

5. Results. Did you get any good from listening to the speech? Did it give information, entertainment, inspiration?

6. What parts of the speech will you remember tomorrow? Was there anything in the speech which you will remember for so much as a week?

Apply these simple tests to any speech and you, as a listener, will gain more from it and you will be able, as evaluator, to give more helpful comments.

(Sept. 1959, pp. 28-29)

HE ASKED FOR IT, BUT HE COULDN'T TAKE IT

You will find the story in the Gospels (Mark 10:17-21, Luke 18:18, Matthew 19:16) and it will pay you to read it as an example of how to seek evaluation, and then fail to profit by it.

The young man came to Jesus, saying, "Good Master, what shall I do to inherit eternal life?"

The Master gave him a direct answer, but the man did not like it. Perhaps he, like many of us, asked for criticism, hoping to receive a compliment. Jesus went to the bottom of the matter and told him the truth. The man had asked a fair question, and he was entitled to an honest opinion.

He must have been a man of attractive personality, for Mark says, "Then Jesus, beholding him, loved him, and said unto him, 'One thing thou lackest; go thy way, sell whatsoever thou hast, and give to the poor, and thou shalt have treasure in heaven; and come, take up the cross, and follow me.' "

The Master saw possibilities in this man, and desired him for a follower, but realized that such a man, carrying the burden of his great wealth, could never be a true disciple until he got rid of his hindrance. His criticism was searching and painful, but sincere. If the inquirer had followed the advice of his evaluator, he might have done great things. As it was, he dropped out of sight and was not heard from further.

He asked for criticism, but when he got it, he simply couldn't take it. He demonstrated one of the three customary reactions to criticism.

Some people, on being evaluated, get mad. They resent the criticism. Others don't believe it. They say, "That's what you think! Well, I don't agree with you. I don't have to accept your suggestion."

But others, wiser and more appreciative, say, "Thank you for the suggestion. It hadn't occurred to me before that I needed to change my ways in that direction, but I see what you mean, and I shall do something about it."

It is the person of the third class who gets the value out of evaluation, or criticism. He accepts it gratefully and studies to see how he can apply it to the best purpose. Even though it deflates his ego, he examines it and tests it.

Like the young man in the story, most of us have favorite weaknesses to which we cling. Either we enjoy the objectionable characteristic, or we think it distinguishes us, or we are unwilling to admit the flaw in our personality. The alcoholic victim knows that strong drink is poison to him, but he does not make the effort to give it up. Many of us are like that with other bad habits and destructive characteristics. It is easier to get along with them than to correct them.

Criticism, whether given in friendship or in malice, can be one of the most constructive elements in life for us. Its value depends altogether on how we accept it and how we use it. The worst way to receive it is to be angry about it. The next worst way is to ignore it. The one best way is to listen to it, study it, and then use it.

The young man asked for criticism. Perhaps he was conscious of a weakness, and wanted someone to relieve his worry. Perhaps he felt that he was so good that he deserved compliments, and thus he wanted to show off before the others. In either case, he asked for it, and he got it. But he couldn't take it.

Here is a Biblical character for us not to imitate. Whenever we receive criticism, whether of our speech or of our conduct in general, the intelligent thing to do is to listen to the criticism, evaluate it from all angles, and then apply it for our own good.

Never "get mad" at your critic. Never fight your evaluator. Never disregard his suggestion, however unreasonable it seems. There may be in it some grain of truth which will help you, if you are wise enough to accept it and try it on yourself for size.

But don't ask for criticism unless you can take it.

(Sept. 1953, pp. 1-2)

SIMPLE TO IMPROVE

When you have made a speech, what do you want from your audience?

More especially, what do you want from your evaluator?

The most important point for you is this: Did I make the sale? Did I accomplish my purpose?

Almost as important is this: Did I make the sale so that the audience enjoyed being sold? Did I give them pleasure or satisfaction along with the facts and arguments I presented?

A third comment which will help you, if you can get it, is this: What can I do in future speeches to make my work still more effective? How can I make my delivery or my argument more acceptable to the listeners?

If your evaluator will answer these three questions for you, he will give you the greatest possible aid—the most useful evaluation. Even the least experienced listener can answer on the first two points. He may know nothing about speech techniques, but he knows whether or not you "sold" him on your proposition, and whether he enjoyed listening to you.

If your evaluator is more experienced in listening and analyzing, he can give you suggestions for improvement.

Of course you wish to avoid mannerisms and procedures which interfere with effective communication of ideas, but you are not nearly so much concerned about the little matters of minor importance as you are about the real accomplishment of purpose.

Try this plan for yourself, as you listen to speakers on all occasions. Ask yourself the three basic questions about the speaker and his speech:

1. Did he accomplish his purpose?

2. Did I enjoy listening to the speech?

3. How could he do better next time?

Try it in your club. Use the simple formula as you evaluate others. You may be a better evaluator than you thought.

(Jan. 1953, pp. 6-7)

Founder Ralph C. Smedley appearing before
the Oklahoma City Toastmasters Club on
October 23, 1946.

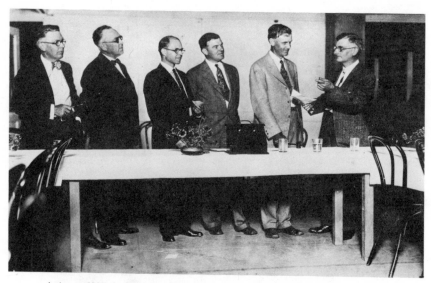

In August, 1927, the first joint meeting of Toastmasters clubs was held in Santa Ana at the invitation of Ralph Smedley. The men made speeches to each other at this meeting and decided to form a simple federation for mutual benefit. Meeting with Smedley, right, that night were representatives of Toastmasters clubs in Anaheim, Fullerton, Santa Ana, Los Angeles and Ontario, California

Founder Ralph Smedley poses in front of a statue of Nathan Hale on the campus of Yale University during a trip in 1947. With him is Leonard Fish, a local Toastmaster.

Ralph Smedley operates the addressograph machine in 1950.

In 1955, California's Governor Goodwin J. Knight signs a proclamation making August 17th "Toastmasters Day" throughout the state. The day marked the opening of the 24th annual International Convention in Los Angeles. Looking on is John W. Haynes, International president in 1955-56.

Dr. Smedley receives the key to the City of San Francisco from Mayor George Christopher during the International Convention in 1959.

Until 1962, the home office of Toastmasters International was in the first floor of the right wing, and the basement, of this building.

Toastmasters assembled for the groundbreaking of the new World Headquarters building in April, 1961. Dr. Smedley and President George J. Mucey turned the first spadefuls of earth.

Executive Director Maurice Forley, President Herman Hoche and Dr. Smedley inspect the progress of the World Headquarters building in November, 1961.

Dr. Smedley and Executive Director Maurice Forley look over the grounds at the newly completed World Headquarters building in October, 1962.

Dr. Smedley speaks at dedication ceremonies for World Headquarters.

Dr. Smedley attends a banquet in Glasgow, Scotland (1953).

In 1960, Dr. Smedley visited Washington, D.C., where he met with Vice President Richard M. Nixon and U.S. Representative James Utt.

Dr. Smedley receives an unusual birthday card from Westinghouse Club 2667-40 (1964).

Dr. Smedley addresses a Toastmasters gathering in Columbus, Ohio (1951).

Ralph Smedley stands with his students outside Caledonia School near Bellflower, Illinois (1901).

Yours, for Better Speeches,
Ralph C. Smedley

Aphorisms and *Precepts*

Within Dr. Smedley's writings are many sayings and statements which will find their way into history. As his material becomes more available, writers and speakers will find a wealth of wisdom, inspiration, and learning. One hundred of the several hundred quotations worthy of special mention have been selected for inclusion here. For some basis of reference, these have been placed under broad headings.

ADMONITIONS

Whatever your grade or position, if you know how and when to speak, and when to remain silent, your chances of real success are proportionately increased.

———

Be sure to have your mind dressed in its best when it goes out on parade.

———

The way you stand and walk is an index of your character.

———

There must always be some degree of intelligence mixed with the perseverance.

———

You can profit by the wisdom of others, and you can give them full credit.

———

You must be a dictator to your mind.

———

Don't sacrifice your dignity for the sake of being a "common" man.

———

Sometimes it pays to make yourself ridiculous, just to prove that you can.

———

The greater the obstacle, the greater glory we have in overcoming it.

CRITICISM

Criticism: A process of evaluation and appraisal for the purpose of improvement.

A critic has a right to find fault only so long as he is prepared to offer a way to deal with the fault he finds.

Faultfinding without suggestions for improvement is a waste of time.

Speech practice without criticism or audience reaction loses half its value.

We gain skill by practice, and we improve by heeding our evaluators.

Evaluation is involved in every phase of your life, for: *Evaluation is Everywhere.*

The true test of a speech is in the reaction of the whole audience, not of a single evaluator.

I do not like to be shouted at unless danger threatens.

My favorite aversion is the "grunt"—the "ah" and the "err-r" with which many speakers fill in the gaps between their words.

Circumstances always modify rules.

It would be very dull if we all talked alike.

●

FEAR
Fear is one of Nature's best gifts to man.

———

Knowledge inspires self-confidence, and knowledge plus confidence will overcome fear of the audience.

———

The unprepared speaker has a right to be scared.

———

Fear of the audience results from a sense of ignorance or insufficiency.

●

GROUPS
You are not a real member of a group until you take your part in a conversation.

———

There is value in the comparison of ideas and experiences, and through the sharing of ideas, progress is made.

———

Everyone wants to feel himself an integral part of something active, vital, worthwhile.

———

The deepest joy belonging comes as one learns to cooperate and contribute and help.

●

LANGUAGE

Language does change by usage, and one generation is shocked by the speech habits of another.

———

When many people give a certain meaning to a word, that word begins to take on that meaning, in spite of all the protests of the purists.

Change is an element of life, and so long as a language is living and in use, change is inevitable.

It is not the size of words that counts, but the clearness with which they represent your thoughts.

Any word becomes a bad word when used too often.

●

LEADERSHIP

Self-expression is one of the first steps towards leadership. Sometimes a man gets hold of an idea, and it shapes his whole life.

The well-balanced, intelligent speaker is the natural leader in any group of which he is a part.

Our responsibilities are defined by our opportunities.

Imagination takes the common place and glorifies it.

●

LISTENING

Real communication is impossible without listening.

Learning to make a speech is important, but almost equally so is learning to listen critically, analytically, and then to give the speaker the benefit.

Too many of us listen with our prejudices rather than with our intelligence.

●

MEMORY

You can control your thoughts, and you can build a dependable memory, but you can't do it by merely wishing for it.

Much of our forgetting results from failure to get clearly in mind the name or fact to be remembered.

The speaker never knows how much of what he says will be remembered, nor how long that memory will last.

PUBLIC SPEAKING

The first result of speech training is *self-discovery*.

The first thing is to have something to say that is worth saying.

The ability to approach an audience in a friendly style is partly a gift of nature, and partly a cultivated art.

If you would make your speeches attractive, impressive, and easily remembered, illuminate them with good illustrations.

People are people, whether on the platform or in the audience.

We can be friends even though you are making a speech.

People will listen to the man with a message—if he knows how to deliver it.

For effective speaking, try to talk *with* your audience.

If you need notes when you speak, use them without hesitation or apology, but use them right.

A speaker cannot hope to convince his hearers if he lacks conviction.

If the speaker does not get stirred up, neither will his audience.

———————

The speaker may be a good show-off, but he can't hold an audience without a message.

———————

Many public speeches could be omitted without great public loss.

———————

Make each joke pay its own way as a contributing factor to the success of the speech.

———————

Any personal characteristic or habit which makes the speech more effective is a good mannerism.

———————

Variety in experience is needed.

———————

The fact which you know by personal experience beats a dozen which you may have borrowed from others.

———————

I am personally allergic to the efforts to select any speech or speaker as "the best."

———————

There are no absolutes in public speaking.

●

PURPOSE

The speaker must know his purpose and how he is going to achieve it.

———————

Purpose determines the good, marks the path, and furnishes the motion power.

———————

A speech without a specific purpose is like a journey without a destination.

Every speech must have a point, an objective, a clear purpose, *and* a conclusion.

Any speech worth making leaves the hearers with a consciousness of something accomplished, something gained.

The target, or destination, determines the style of the speech.

When you speak, never leave your audience in doubt as to what you think they should do.

Merely to make a speech is not enough. The speech must mean something—lead to something—stir up someone to know or do or attempt something.

●

SELLING

All talking is selling and all selling involves talking.

The success of our speech depends on how well we sell the idea.

Every speech which has a real purpose becomes a selling talk.

●

SPEECH

Civilization and speech have grown up together.

Speech is much more than merely standing before an audience and saying something.

The startling discovery has been made that talking on the telelephone is really a form of public speaking and can lead to improvement in business and in personal prestige.

———————

A speech is great in proportion to the greatness of the occasion which calls it forth, the greatness of the speaker as a man, the importance of the theme and the extent of the results it accomplishes.

———————

Great is the power of the spoken word, when it is spoken in truth, by one whose life supports what he says.

———————

In the beginning, I was convinced that the way to learn to make speeches was by making speeches.

●

STORIES

A pertinent story or a picturesque word is remembered when the argument has been forgotten.

———————

The time to tell a story is the time when it is appropriate.

———————

A story must pay its own way by contributing to the thought.

———————

Select the stories you tell; don't dabble in dirt.

———————

Some people seem to be born bores, while others learn the art by experience.

THINKING

The real thinker becomes the master of those who merely think they think.

———————

Thinking and studying are hard work. Indolence shrinks from them.

———————

I know of no method whereby we can overcome the reluctance of men to think and plan and work to a purpose.

———————

The greatest speakers have usually been remarkable for the abundance of their ideas and their economy of words.

———————

Life is full of intriguing problems to be discussed. No one need waste time on unimportant themes.

———————

Life takes on a different aspect when you step out with decision and purpose.

———————

Our past prepares us to meet the challenges of the future.

———————

One of the best ways to discipline one's thinking is to put it in writing.

●

TOASTMASTERS

The Toastmasters Club is fundamentally an educational organization.

———————

Toastmasters is learning through doing and improving through criticism.

My amazement at our educational achievement is equaled by my gratified surprise at the results we have produced.

●

UNDERSTANDING

All speech is for communication, and there is no possibility of communication unless people understand.

Understanding comes through communication, and through understanding we find the way to peace.

Most of the conflicts and disagreements among men result from misunderstanding.

Depend on this one fact: The future of mankind, peace, progress and prosperity must be finally determined by the extent to which men can be brought to a state of common and honest understanding.

Understanding leads to the revealing of new ideas to be understood and used.

We need fewer rules on detail and better understanding of general principles.

The principles of communication do not change.